A Divine
Light

OTHER BOOKS IN THE LEADERS IN ACTION SERIES

A Place to Stand:
The Word of God in the Life of Martin Luther
Gene E. Veith

All Things for Good:
The Steadfast Fidelity of Stonewall Jackson
J. Steven Wilkins

Beyond Stateliest Marble:
The Passionate Femininity of Anne Bradstreet
by Douglas Wilson

Call of Duty: The Sterling Nobility of Robert E. Lee
by J. Steven Wilkins

Carry a Big Stick: The Uncommon Heroism of Theodore Roosevelt
by George Grant

For Kirk and Covenant: The Stalwart Courage of John Knox
by Douglas Wilson

Forgotten Founding Father: The Heroic Legacy of George Whitefield
by Stephen Mansfield

Give Me Liberty:
The Uncompromising Statesmanship of Patrick Henry
by David J. Vaughan

Never Give In: The Extraordinary Character of Winston Churchill
by Stephen Mansfield

Not a Tame Lion: The Spiritual Legacy of C. S. Lewis
by Terry W. Glaspey

The Pillars of Leadership
by David J. Vaughan

Statesman and Saint: The Principled Politics of William Wilberforce
by David Vaughan

Then Darkness Fled: The Liberating Wisdom of Booker T. Washington
by Stephen Mansfield

A Divine Light

THE SPIRITUAL LEADERSHIP OF JONATHAN EDWARDS

LEADERS
IN
ACTION

DAVID VAUGHAN

DAVID VAUGHAN, GENERAL EDITOR

CUMBERLAND HOUSE
NASHVILLE, TENNESSEE

A Divine Light
Published by Cumberland House Publishing, Inc.
431 Harding Industrial Drive
Nashville, Tennessee 37211

Cover design by Gore Studio, Inc., Nashville, Tennessee

Library of Congress Cataloging-in-Publication Data

Vaughan, David J., 1955–
  A divine light : the spiritual leadership of Jonathan Edwards /
David J. Vaughan.
      p. cm. — (Leaders in action)
  Includes bibliographical references and index.
  ISBN-13: 978-1-58182-545-9 (hardcover)
  ISBN-10: 1-58182-545-5 (hardcover)
  1. Edwards, Jonathan, 1703–1758. 2. Christian leadership. I. Title.
II. Series.
BX7260.E3V377 2007
285.8092—dc22
[B]   2006035044

2 3 4 5 6 7 8 9 10—10 09 08 07

To my family,
may we learn to walk
in the divine llight

CONTENTS

Acknowledgments   9

Chronology of Edwards's Life   11

PART 1: THE LIFE OF JONATHAN EDWARDS

The Puritan Hope   19

Meeting God at Yale   26

Ministry and Marriage   39

Receiving the Mantle   46

Breaking Up the Fallow Ground   56

Whitefield and the Great Awakening   65

In Defense of Revival   78

Controversy and Dismissal   88

Frontier Theologian   101

An Unhappy Providence   115

PART 2: THE CHARACTER OF JONATHAN EDWARDS

Books   123

Study   127

Discipline   132

Consecration   136

Determination   139

Spirituality   143
Humility   147
Holiness   153
Duty   157
Love for God   162
Love for Man   166
Ministry   169
Christlikeness   174
Civic Leadership   178
Preaching   183
Family   186
Spiritual Disciplines   189
Experiential Religion   193
Sovereignty   197
Gloria Dei   201

PART 3: THE LEGACY OF JONATHAN EDWARDS

Vindication   207
To Future Generations   210
Life and Letters   214
Memorial   217
The Lessons of Leadership   219
Notes   221
Bibliography   231
Index   235

Acknowledgments

O F THE many friends who have supported me over the years, special thanks goes to the staff of Liberty Christian Church: David and Katherine Volz; Bryan and Debbie Short; Mike and Andrea Bond; Rob and Jeannie Witty; and Sammy and Judy Grisham. To the members of Liberty, I can only say that it is a privilege to serve you as pastor. My prayer is that God will visit us with a revival like the Great Awakening.

Thanks also to George Grant, the former editor of the Leaders in Action series, for launching my writing career, and to Ron Pitkin, president of Cumberland House, for seeing the value of biography for leadership training.

Most important, I am indebted to my wife, Diane, and my four children—Hannah, Lydia, Ethan, and Adam. May each of you learn the secret of consecration.

CHRONOLOGY

1703   October 5: Edwards born at East Windsor, Conn.

1708–9   Edwards has first "religious experience" during revival in father's church.

1713   Edwards writes paper attacking materialism.

1716   Earliest letter to sister (May 10); essay "Of Insects" supposedly written at this time; September: enrolls in Yale.

1720   Graduates from Yale with his bachelor's degree. Stays at Yale as graduate student until 1722.

1721   Writes "Of Being." Spring: conversion experience.

1722   August: Edwards becomes minister of small Presbyterian church in New York. Stays only eight months. Develops "Resolutions."

1723   Writes "The Mind" and "Apostrophe to Sarah Pierrepont." April: leaves New York parish and spends summer with parents. September: returns to Yale, receives MA degree.

1724   May: appointed tutor at Yale. Takes up residence in June.

1725   Writes "Beauty of the World." September: Edwards suffers severe illness, lasting three months; never recovers former strength.

1726   August: receives call to Northampton. September: resigns as tutor at Yale.

1727   February 15: ordained as associate pastor of Northampton congregation under the pastorate of Solomon Stoddard, his maternal grandfather. July 28: twenty-three-year-old Edwards marries seventeen-year-old Sarah Pierrepont. Sarah's father was a founder of Yale and framer of the Saybrook Platform.

1728   Writes "Images of Divine Things."

1729   February: Solomon Stoddard dies. Edwards becomes pastor of Northampton. Spring: Edwards's health breaks down.

1731   July 8: Edwards gives "public lecture" in Boston, published as *God Glorified in Man's Dependence*.

1734   Edwards preaches controversial sermons on justification and is criticized by the Williams side of his family. December: revival begins in Northampton. Preaches "A Divine and Supernatural Light" and "Discourses on Various Subjects."

1735   April: revival reaches height; Joseph Hawley, Edwards's uncle, commits suicide. Fall: Edwards takes vacation for health reasons; travels to New York and New Jersey and meets Tennents.

1737   Fall: publication in London of *Faithful Narrative*.

1738   Preaches "Charity and Its Fruits"; publishes *Discourses on Various Subjects*.

1739   Writes "A History of the Work of Redemption." Composes "Personal Narrative." George Whitefield arrives in America.

1740   October 17: Whitefield visits Edwards and preaches at Northampton.

1741   July: revival progresses. Edwards preaches famous sermon "Sinners in the Hands of an Angry God" at Enfield. September: Edwards at Yale commencement; Samuel Hopkins first hears Edwards here. Edwards preaches New

Haven sermon "Distinguishing Marks." December: Edwards on "missionary tour." Hopkins arrives at parsonage, stays six to seven months.

1742   January: Edwards preaches at Leicester. February: returns to Northampton to find Sarah "revived." Summer: revival begins to subside. Publication of *Some Thoughts on Present Revival.*

1743   Charles Chauncy, pastor of First Church of Boston, publishes *Seasonable Thoughts etc.* against revival.

1744   Troubles begin at Northampton: bad book case, dispute over salary. October: start of International Union.

1746   Publication of *Treatise on Religious Affections.*

1747   Publication of *A Humble Attempt, etc.* May 28: David Brainerd arrives at Northampton. October 9: Brainerd dies.

1748   February: Edwards's daughter Jerusha dies.

1749   Publication of *Life of Brainerd* and *An Humble Inquiry, etc.*

1750   June 22: Edwards dismissed from Northampton pastorate. July: farewell sermon. December: Edwards receives call to Stockbridge missionary settlement.

1751   August 8: Edwards officially installed at Stockbridge. Conflict with Williams family.

1752   November: publication of *Misrepresentations Corrected.*

1754   Publication of *Freedom of the Will.* July–December: Edwards seriously ill with fever.

1755   Edwards writes *Nature of True Virtue* and *End for Which God Created the World;* both published posthumously.

1755–63 Seven Years' War between England and France (known as French and Indian War in the colonies).

1757   September 24: Edwards's son-in-law, Aaron Burr, president

of the College of New Jersey (Princeton), dies. Edwards
called to be president.

1758   *Original Sin.* February 16: Edwards installed as president
of Princeton. February 23: Edwards inoculated for smallpox. March 22: Edwards dies from smallpox. Six months
later his wife, Sarah, dies. Both are buried at Princeton.

A Divine
Light

Part 1

The Life of Jonathan Edwards

We cannot take leave of Edwards, without testifying the whole extent of the reverence that we bear him. The American divine affords, perhaps, the most wondrous example in modern time, of one who stood richly gifted both in natural and spiritual discernment—and we know not what most to admire in him, whether the deep philosophy that issued from his pen, or the humble and child-like piety that issued from his pulpit.
　　　　　　　　　　　　　—Thomas Chalmers

Jonathan Edwards, saint and metaphysician, revivalist and theologian, stands out as the one figure of real greatness in the intellectual life of colonial America.
　　　　　　　　　　　　　—Benjamin B. Warfield

It is the spirit of a truly godly man, to prefer God before all other things, either in heaven or on earth.
　　　　　　　　　　　　　—Jonathan Edwards

THE PURITAN HOPE

*T*HE GREAT EXPERIMENT OF American theocracy was coming to a close at the time of Jonathan Edwards's birth in 1703. The fire of his Puritan forefathers was cooling to a smoldering ember. As the zeal of genuine piety waned, many decried the decline in religion and bewailed the spiritual apathy that pervaded the colonies. In 1706, Cotton Mather, like the Old Testament prophet Jeremiah, poured out his lamentation: "It is confessed by all who know anything of the matter . . . that there is a general and an horrible decay of Christianity, among the professors of it. . . . The modern Christianity is too generally but a very spectre, scarce a shadow of the ancient. Ah! Sinful nation. Ah! Children that are corrupters: what have your hands done!"[1]

Mather was not alone in describing the depressing picture of colonial carnality. "The ministerial utterances of the period—from the pulpit and press—were equally gloomy."[2] Richard Webster repined: "A vast change was visible in the churches of New England: the discipline was relaxed, the doctrine was diluted, and the preaching tame and spiritless."[3] Just a year before Edwards's birth, Increase Mather wistfully recalled the glory of earlier days: "You that are aged, and can remember what New England was fifty years ago, that saw these churches in their first glory, is there not a sad decay and diminution of that glory! How is the gold become dim!"[4] There is no doubt that religion had sunk to a new low in the colonies. As one historian noted:

> Taken as a whole, no century in American religious history has been so barren as the eighteenth. The fire and enthusiasm of Puritanism had died out on both sides of the Atlantic. In this country the inevitable provincialism of the narrow colonial life, the deadening influence of its hard grapple with the rude forces of nature, and the Indian and Canadian wars rendered each generation less actively religious than its predecessor; and, while New England shone as compared with the spiritual deadness of Old England in the years preceding Wesley, the old fervor and sense of a national mission were gone, conscious conversion, once so common, was unusual, and religion was becoming more formal and external.[5]

In addition to the reasons just mentioned, other factors facilitated the decline of Puritan piety. One was the development of the Half-Way Covenant. As the second generation of Puritans grew up, many were converted but could not offer explicit accounts of their conversion experience, which was a basic requirement for full membership in the church in New England. As "noncommunicant" members, they could neither vote nor partake of the Lord's Supper. And what about their children? Could noncommunicant parents present their children for baptism? In 1656 a group of New England clergymen debated the question in Boston. Their solution, known as the Half-Way Covenant, stated that children of noncommunicants could be baptized, provided that the children led a morally upright life and agreed to profess the church covenant before their congregation. These children essentially became "halfway" church members, like their parents. Later, as adults, their children were baptized under the same conditions. To compound the compromise, Jonathan Edwards's grandfather Solomon Stoddard of Northampton advanced the idea that these halfway members should be offered full communion, believing that the Lord's Supper was a means of conversion. Thus many Congregational churches were comprised of members who had made no profession of saving faith. The sad but inevitable result was the decay of spiritual vitality.

Edwards's own parents were, however, a notable exception to the prevailing decline. His father, Timothy Edwards, was a man of fair complexion, strong build, lively temperament, and genuine godliness. As pastor of the church in East Windsor, Connecticut, Timothy Edwards's ministry experienced several seasons of revival. As Jonathan wrote later: "My honoured father's parish has in times past been a place favoured with mercies of this [awakening] nature, above any on this western side of

New England, excepting Northampton; there having been four or five seasons of the pouring out of the Spirit to the general awakening of the people there since my father's settlement amongst them."[6]

Some years earlier, when Timothy had been a student at Harvard, he had met his future bride, Esther Stoddard. She was a woman of grace and wit: tall, affable, and according to some, superior to her husband in "native vigour of understanding."[7] Her family was one of the leading families in the Connecticut Valley due to the influence of her father, the Reverend Solomon Stoddard, who began a long and powerful ministry at Northampton in 1669. In the course of his extended pastorate (1669–1729), the city of Northampton became the largest settlement of inland Massachusetts, and Stoddard's reputation as a preacher grew with the city.

On November 6, 1694, Timothy Edwards married Esther Stoddard at Northampton, and a week later they moved to East Windsor, where Timothy had been called to preach. After an initial probation period, he was ordained pastor in March 1695. Since the general court had only recently authorized the organization of a separate parish, the people were busy constructing a new meetinghouse and parsonage. Timothy's father, Richard Edwards, covered the cost of the brick and hewn timber and purchased some surrounding farmland for the newlyweds.

Here, in a two-story log parsonage, Jonathan Edwards was born on October 5, 1703. The only son of eleven children (four sisters preceded him and six sisters followed), Jonathan was of special interest to his father. Since there was no school in fledgling East Windsor, Timothy Edwards schooled his children at home, and like other New England ministers, he often took in students from the surrounding area. Having graduated from Harvard with both bachelor's and master's degrees, he was eminently qualified to do so. In addition to a thorough knowledge of the Bible and Reformed theology, he excelled in the Greek and Latin classics and had a fondness for poetry and the study of nature.

Under his father's tutelage, Jonathan began the study of Latin at the age of six; he had a reading knowledge of Latin, Greek, and Hebrew by the time he was thirteen. He also learned to study with a pen in his hand at all times. This habit, begun at an early stage of his life, taught Edwards to think clearly and logically and to record his reflections on many important subjects. The father's love of nature was also passed on to the son. It was not uncommon for Jonathan to lie on the grass outside his home and watch butterflies or moths or to stroll in the woods and patiently observe the operations of "flying" spiders. Consequently, at the age of eleven, the young naturalist wrote a three-thousand-word "scientific" paper on spiders. Some years later, he reworked the original and submitted it to the Royal Society of London. Although it was never published, it illustrates Edwards's precocious gifts of observation and analysis. The young man's genius was also reflected in the well-known anecdote of H. C. McCook, who believed himself the first person to make certain observations on flying spiders; he was chagrined to learn that Edwards had anticipated his work by 160 years.

More important, Jonathan learned a high view of God, Christ, the Bible, and Christian ministry from his parents.

His home was the setting for many devout prayers and divine precepts. Both parents set godly examples that reinforced their instruction. Their hearts' desire was that their son "might be filled with the Holy Spirit; from a child know the Holy Scriptures; and be great in the sight of the Lord."[8]

Timothy was an earnest preacher whose ministry witnessed the blessing of God's Spirit by several seasons of "reviving of religion." During one of these general awakenings, the Holy Spirit touched Jonathan himself. He later wrote:

> I had a variety of concerns and exercises about my soul from my childhood; but I had two more remarkable seasons of awakening before I met with that change by which I was brought to those new dispositions, and that new sense of things, that I have since had. The first time was when I was a boy, some years before I went to College, at a time of remarkable awakening in my father's congregation. I was very much affected for many months, and concerned about the things of religion, and my soul's salvation. . . . I used to pray five times a day in secret, and to spend much time in religious talk with other boys; and used to meet with them to pray together. I experienced I know not what kind of delight in religion. My mind was much engaged in it, and had much self-righteous pleasure, and it was my delight to abound in religious duties.[9]

Jonathan and some schoolmates built a prayer booth in a nearby swamp, and he would often go to secret places in the woods by himself to pray. Although he was "much affected" at this time, Edwards believed that his real conversion came later. Eventually his "convictions and affections wore off," and he "went on in the ways of sin."[10]

Nevertheless, his father had fortified him intellectually and stimulated him spiritually. He was ready to venture into the world as a young scholar. And at the tender age of thirteen, Jonathan Edwards headed for Yale.

MEETING GOD AT YALE

*E*DWARDS JOINED THE COLLEGIATE School of Connecticut (later renamed Yale) in the autumn of 1716. The school charter, drawn up in 1701, succinctly stated the goal and vision of its founders: "to promote the power and piety of religion, and the best edification of these New England Churches."[11] In contrast to liberal-leaning Harvard, the Connecticut school was committed to conserving the Puritan heritage of New England. Thus its founders filled the library with the works of weighty reformers like Johann Heinrich Alsted, Johannes Wollebius, and other Dutch and Swiss theologians.

In its infancy, the college had no official name. It also had no official location, a fact that led to controversy among the students, professors, and trustees. When Edwards began his studies, there were student bodies at four sites: Hartford, New Haven, Saybrook, and Wethersfield.

In the midst of much wrangling between the students' parents and the school's trustees, it was decided in October 1716 that the permanent site of the college would be New Haven. Despite this decision, Edwards and a group of students stayed at Wethersfield under the instruction of Elisha Williams, who was Edwards's half-cousin.[12] Two years later, the general assembly of Connecticut, in October 1718, resolved the tension, and the Wethersfield students were moved to the New Haven campus in the summer of 1719. Thus Edwards was not present for the commencement of September 1718, when the school was officially named Yale.

The Yale curriculum was a blend of traditional Reformed theology and what was then called the "new learning"—the philosophy of Robert Boyle, René Descartes, John Locke, and Isaac Newton. In general, the four-year course of study covered ancient languages (Greek, Hebrew, and Latin), logic, natural science, higher mathematics, and astronomy. Writing home to his father, Jonathan requested assistance in procuring some of his texts and supplies: "I have inquired of Mr. [Timothy] Cutler what books we shall need of the next year. He answered, he would have me to get against that time, Alstead's [John Alsted's] Geometry and [Petrus] Gassendus's Astronomy; with which I would entreat you to get a pair of dividers, or mathematician's compasses, and a scale, which are absolutely necessary in order to learning mathematics; and also the Art of Thinking, which, I am persuaded, would be no less profitable than the other necessary."[13]

Since the primary aim of the college was to train godly ministers and to promote the welfare of New England's churches, courses in divinity, homiletics, New Testament Greek, and the Hebrew Psalter were also required. Moreover, students had to memorize the Westminster Catechism and the theological theses (*Marrow of Sacred Theology*) of William Ames.

The spiritual life of the students was encouraged also. "Orders and Appointments" for the students included the following regimen:

> Every student shall exercise himself in reading Holy Scriptures by himself everyday that the word of Christ may dwell in him richly. . . . All students shall avoid the profanation of God's holy name, attributes, Word and ordinances and the Holy Sabbath, and shall carefully attend all public assemblies for divine worship. . . . All undergraduates shall publicly repeat sermons in the hall in their course, and . . . be constantly examined on Sabbaths at evening prayer.[14]

Edwards's education served him well. Being naturally precocious and curious, he studied diligently and ranked first in his class when his undergraduate work concluded. In September 1720, he gave the farewell oration at the college commencement. But instead of heading home, he stayed at Yale to pursue a master's degree.

The years between 1720 and 1726 were critical in Edwards's intellectual and spiritual development. As a graduate student (1720–22), and later as a tutor (1724–26), Edwards's intellectual horizons expanded greatly. He avidly read the new learning. His favorite philosopher at the time was John Locke, whose *Essay Concerning Human Under-*

standing gave him more pleasure "than the most greedy miser finds when gathering up handfuls of silver and gold."[15]

Edwards continued to study with a pen in his hand, and during this time he began a lifelong practice of keeping notebooks with such headings as "Natural Philosophy," "The Mind," and "Miscellanies." In his "Notes on Natural Science," Edwards demonstrated an understanding and appreciation of Isaac Newton, not to mention the genius of his own scientific mind. He discussed, for instance, the definition of an atom and its constitution, gravity, repulsion and attraction, light, color, planets, comets, the growth of trees, lightning, the twinkling of fixed stars, how water freezes and evaporates, etc. In another essay, "Of Being," he argued for the inevitability of existence from the inconceivability of nonexistence.

A notebook titled "Catalogues" listed the books Edwards had read or hoped to read. Of the 690 entries, 452 were on religious topics. From this list it is clear that his favorite authors were the older Puritans: William Perkins, Richard Sibbes, Thomas Manton, John Flavel, John Owen, and Stephen Charnock, among others. He was also well versed with John Calvin, Francis Turretin, and Peter van Mastricht; the latter, he said, being "better than any other book in the world, excepting the Bible, in my opinion."[16]

Edwards's spiritual growth was, of course, even more consequential than his intellectual development. Although he had been touched by the Spirit of God when he was a child, Edwards now experienced a crisis of faith. Despite his efforts to live godly, he found that he repeatedly suffered "inward struggles and conflicts" of temptation. He began to

see that true Christianity was more than external conformity to a set of rules; he recognized the need for a deep and
abiding change in his heart. Thus he began to seek salvation
fervently. He journaled, "I was indeed brought to seek salvation in a manner that I never was before; I felt a spirit to
part with all things in the world for an interest in Christ."[17]

Like the "wretched man" of Romans 7, Edwards
ceased his efforts and prayed to God for deliverance. In
the late spring of 1721 his prayer was answered. He later
wrote in his *Personal Narrative* that he found the joy and
peace of salvation while reading 1 Timothy 1:17:

> The instance that I remember of that sort of inward,
> sweet delight in God and divine things that I have lived
> much in since, was on reading those words, I Tim. 1:17.
> "Now unto the King eternal, immortal, invisible, the only
> wise God, be honour and glory for ever and ever, Amen."
> As I read the words, there came into my soul, and was as
> it were diffused through it, a sense of the glory of the Di-
> vine Being; a new sense, quite different from any thing I
> ever experienced before. . . . I thought with myself, how
> excellent a Being that was, and how happy I should be, if
> I might enjoy that God, and be rapt up in him in heaven,
> and be as it were swallowed up in him for ever![18]

From then on, Edwards began to have new "apprehensions and ideas" about Christ, redemption, and salvation:
"An inward, sweet sense of these things, at times, came
into my heart; and my soul was led away in pleasant views
and contemplations of them." Edwards was enraptured
with Christ and spent many hours "reading and meditating

on Christ, on the beauty and excellency of his person, and the lovely way of salvation by free grace." Song of Solomon became one of his favorite books of the Bible. While meditating upon it, a sense of divine things "would often of a sudden kindle up . . . a sweet burning in my heart; an ardor of soul, that I know not how to express."[19]

That summer Edwards returned home and shared his spiritual experience with his father. After their conversation, which "much affected" the younger Edwards, he went into his father's pasture to meditate. "And as I was walking there, and looking up on the sky and clouds, there came into my mind so sweet a sense of the glorious *majesty* and *grace* of God, that I know not how to express—I seemed to see them both in a sweet conjunction; majesty and meekness joined together." Clearly, Edwards was in the honeymoon glow of his conversion: that sweet and joyous time of experiencing "all things new" in Christ: "The appearance of every thing was altered; there seemed to be, as it were, a calm, sweet cast, or appearance of divine glory, in almost every thing." Even nature was aglow with the glory of God: "God's excellency, his wisdom, his purity and love, seemed to appear in every thing; in the sun, moon, and stars; in the clouds, and blue sky; in the grass, flowers, tree; in the water and all nature; which used greatly to fix my mind."[20]

While spending that summer at home, for hours he would often contemplate the work of God in creation. He would observe the sky and clouds while "singing forth, with a low voice my contemplations of the Creator and Redeemer." Whereas Edwards formerly had been terrified by thunder, he now rejoiced in it as a manifestation of

God's powerful and majestic voice. Now, whenever a storm approached, he would perch where he could best view the coming glory, and while gazing up at God's fireworks, he would "break forth in singing or chanting" his meditations.[21]

When Edwards returned to Yale in the autumn of 1721, he was not content to be a nominal Christian. He wrote: "I felt then great satisfaction, as to my good state; but that did not content me. I had vehement longings of soul after God and Christ, and after more holiness, wherewith my heart seemed to be full, and ready to break."[22] He was determined to devote himself to God. Indeed, this is the key to understanding his power and life. And this is undoubtedly the reason why God was to later use Jonathan Edwards as an instrument of revival. His intention to fully consecrate himself to God can be seen in the following resolutions, which he began writing in 1722 while at Yale:

> Being sensible that I am unable to do anything without God's help, I do humbly entreat him by his grace to enable me to keep these Resolutions, so far as they are agreeable to his will, for Christ's sake.
> * Resolved, that I will do whatsoever I think to be most to God's glory, and my own good, profit and pleasure in the whole of my duration [life], without any consideration of the time, whether now, or never so many myriads of ages hence. Resolved to do whatever I think to be my duty and most for the good and advantage of mankind in general. Resolved to do this, whatever difficulties I meet with, how many soever, and how great soever.

- Resolved, never to do any manner of thing, whether in soul or body, less or more, but what tends to the glory of God; not be, nor suffer it, if I can avoid it.
- Resolved, never to do anything, which I should be afraid to do, if it were the last hour of my life.
- Resolved, when I feel pain, to think of the pains of martyrdom, and of hell.
- Resolved, to be endeavoring to find out fit objects of charity and liberality.
- Resolved, to live so, at all times, as I think is best in my devout frames, and when I have clearest notions of things of the gospel, and another world.
- Resolved, to examine carefully, and constantly, what that one thing in me is, which causes me in the least to doubt of the love of God; and to direct all my forces against it.
- Resolved, to strive to my utmost every week to be brought higher in religion, and to a higher exercise of grace, than I was the week before.
- Resolved, never to say anything at all against anybody, but when it is perfectly agreeable to the highest degree of Christian honor, and of love to mankind, agreeable to the lowest humility, and a sense of my own faults and failings, and agreeable to the golden rule.[23]

While Edwards was penning his resolutions, he received a call to preach in New York at a small Presbyterian church. Accordingly, he was licensed for the work of the ministry, ceased his master's studies at Yale, and traveled to New York, where he settled in August 1722.

There, Edwards's early sermons overflowed with his

newfound life in Christ: "When a man is enlightened sav-
ingly by Christ, he is, as it were, brought into a new world."
As he himself had experienced, he now preached that a
new convert now "sees with his own eyes and admires and
is astonished" at the "excellency of religion and the glorious
mysteries of the gospel." He loves Christ more than any
other lover: "There is no such near or intimate conversation
between any other lovers as between Christ and the Christian."[24] This was certainly true of Christ and Edwards. As
he wrote later, his desire for Christ and holiness only intensified in New York: "My sense of divine things seemed
gradually to increase, until I went to preach at New York,
which was about a year and a half after they began; and
while I was there, I felt them, very sensible, in a much
higher degree than I had done before. My longing after God
and holiness, were much increased. Pure and humble, holy
and heavenly, Christianity appeared exceeding amiable to
me." Edwards now "felt a burning desire to be in every
thing a complete Christian; and conformed to the blessed
image of Christ; and that I might live, in all things, according to the pure, sweet and blessed rules of the gospel."[25]

"God and holiness!" "Christ and holiness!" These ideas
were inseparably linked in Edwards's mind and experience. To have the one is to possess the other. Thus holiness is not a burdensome duty; it is the beautiful
condition of the soul in communion with God. In one of
his more eloquent passages, Edwards described it:

Holiness . . . appeared to me to be of a sweet, pleasant,
charming serene, calm nature; which brought an inexpressible purity, brightness, peacefulness and ravishment

to the soul. In other words, that it made the soul like a field or garden of God, with all manner of pleasant flowers; all pleasant, delightful, and undisturbed; enjoying a sweet calm, and the gentle vivifying beams of the sun. The soul of a true Christian, as I then wrote . . . appeared like such a little white flower as we see in the spring of the year; low and humble on the ground, opening its bosom to receive the pleasant beams of the sun's glory; rejoicing as it were in a calm rapture; diffusing around a sweet fragrancy. . . . There is no part of creature holiness, that I had so great a sense of its loveliness, as humility, brokenness of heart and poverty of spirit; and there was nothing that I so earnestly longed for. My heart panted after this—to lie low before God, as in the dust; that I might be nothing, and God might be all.[26]

Edwards's ardent passion for God evoked a decisive act of self-consecration. On the morning of January 12, 1723, he was again alone with God and "solemnly renewed" his self-dedication. Edwards vowed complete self-renunciation and devotion to God. He wrote in his diary:

I have been before God; and have given myself, all that I am and have to God, so that I am not in any respect my own: I can challenge no right in myself, I can challenge no right in this understanding, this will, these affections that are in me; neither have I any right to this body, any of its members: no right to this tongue, these hands nor feet: no right to these senses, these eyes, these ears, this smell or taste. I have given myself clear away, and have not retained anything as my own. I have been to God this morning, and told him that I have given myself *wholly* to him. I have given every power to him; so that for the future I will challenge no right in myself, in any respect. . . . This have I done. And I pray God, for the sake of Christ, to look upon it as a self-dedication; and to receive me now as entirely his own, and deal with me in all respects as such, whether he afflicts me or prospers me, or whatever he pleases to do with me, who am his.[27]

Biographer Iain Murray observed that Edwards's resolutions and diary give us "the key to the understanding of his whole life and future ministry. . . . His endevours after holiness are no more the self-conscious strivings of a moralist: rather they are the response of love to the God who had made him a new creature in Jesus Christ." Sanctification was now a labor of love flowing from "communion with God and fellowship with Christ."[28] Moreover, Edwards's solemn self-dedication was perhaps his most significant private act, for God clearly heard his prayer and employed him as one of his mightiest servants in the history of the church.

Edwards's stay at New York was a time of heaven on earth, but this was cut short by the congregation's lack of funds. His parishioners could afford neither the upkeep of their building nor Edwards's salary. Thus, in April 1723, after only an eight-month pastorate, he departed disconsolate from his little New York flock. "My heart seemed to sink within me," he later wrote, "at leaving the family and city where I had enjoyed so many sweet and pleasant days. . . . As I sailed away, I kept sight of the city as long as I could; and when I was out of sight of it, it would affect me much to look that way, with a kind of melancholy mixed with sweetness."[29]

Throughout the summer of 1723 Edwards preached at various churches and completed his master's thesis. In September he was awarded his degree, being a month shy of his twentieth birthday.[30] He was now being pursued as a pastor and a scholar. While calls were coming from several New England churches where he had preached, Yale offered him a position as a tutor. Edwards's desire, however, was to be in the pulpit. His heart was foremost in the ministry: his new master passion was the study and exposition of God's Word.

Edwards's father, on the other hand, pressed him to return to Yale. His reasons are not known. Perhaps he believed that Jonathan would benefit from the academic environment. Another possibility, however, may have been the recent defection or "apostasy" within the Yale faculty. In 1722, rector Timothy Cutler and tutor Daniel Brown denounced Congregationalism, resigned from Yale, and sought Anglican ordination in England. This event caused great concern at the time and was viewed as evidence of the growing threats of Arminianism and Episcopalianism.[31] The school was foundering and needed brilliant minds like Edwards's "to help repair the shattered prestige of the college."[32] Somewhat reluctantly, Edwards deferred to his father and returned to Yale in June 1724.

The next two years were a spiritual wasteland for Edwards. While he increased in intellectual knowledge, he decreased in spiritual comfort. In his *Personal Narrative,* he sums up his time as tutor by such dismal remarks as "After I went to New Haven, I sunk in religion; my mind being diverted from my eager and violent pursuits after holiness." Later, after a severe illness in September 1725, Edwards observed, "I was again greatly diverted in my mind . . . greatly to the wounding of my soul."[33] Despite his inward struggles, Edwards performed his duties admirably. He and his fellow tutors were later recognized as "the pillar tutors, and the glory of the college. . . . Their tutorial renown was great and excellent."[34]

Fortunately, in August 1726, Edwards received a call to minister as the associate pastor of his maternal grandfather, Solomon Stoddard. A month later, he gladly resigned from Yale and hastened to Northampton.

MINISTRY AND MARRIAGE

*E*DWARDS'S MINISTRY AT NORTHAMPTON began with the brightness of a New England summer sun. Yet a dark storm was stirring just beyond the peaceful horizon. Little did Edwards know that the dissension and strife that one day would poison his ministry were already festering in the soil of peaceful Northampton.

Indeed, it was the rich and fertile soil that first attracted settlers to this fortified village in 1650. Except for a few trades and professions, the majority of the town's inhabitants lived off the land. The men rose at dawn to a simple breakfast of bread and cornmeal pudding, labored until the church bell rang at noon for lunch, then resumed their work till dusk. After a supper of meat, bread, and milk, the typical Northampton family had a time of prayer and Bible reading before going to bed. Life in Northampton was a common round of routines reminiscent of Henry Wadsworth Longfellow's village blacksmith:

> Toiling,—rejoicing,—sorrowing,
> Onward through life he goes;
> Each morning sees some task begin,
> Each evening sees it close;
> Something attempted, something done,
> Has earned a night's repose.[35]

The people of Northampton were knit together by several facts of colonial life: social friendships, common lands, common schools, the need for a militia, and their common worship of God. The daily routine of work was punctuated by the weekly ritual of worship. The Sabbath began on Saturday evening, with worship services on Sunday morning and afternoon. An additional "lecture" was also attended on Thursday afternoons at 2:00 p.m. The form of service included praise from the Bay Psalm Book, pastor-led prayer, and a lengthy sermon (sometimes two hours long).

Between 1670 and 1729, the population of Northampton grew from five hundred to a little more than fifteen hundred, and due to the scarce and expensive land, it became a closed, homogeneous community. Writing some years after his arrival there, Edwards described his new hometown:

> The town of Northampton is about 82 years standing, and has about 200 families; which mostly dwell more compactly together than any town of such a bigness in

these parts of the country. . . . Take the town in general,
and so far as I can judge, they are as rational and understanding a people as most I have been acquainted with:
many of them have been noted for religion, and particularly have been remarkable for their distinct knowledge
in things that relate to heart religion and Christian experience, and their great regards thereto.[36]

Despite the strong communal spirit that had been
forged by hardship and peril, work and worship, the town
and the church had suffered a division based upon social
inequality. While all the men were "freeholders," a few of
the founding families were "proprietors" who held the
reigns of political power, social status, and personal wealth.
Edwards later noted the town's central division:

It has been a very great wound to the church of Northampton, that there has been for forty of fifty years, a sort
of settled division of the people into two parties. . . .
There have been some of the chief men in the town, of
chief authority and wealth, that have been great proprietors of their lands, who have had one party with them.
And the other party, which has commonly been the greatest, have been of those, who have been jealous of them,
apt to envy them, and afraid of their having too much
power and influence in town and church.[37]

As a result, the church at Northampton had suffered a
series of "mighty contests and contentions" long before
Edwards arrived there.

Notwithstanding this dissension, the church agreed

"by a very great majority" to invite Edwards to "settle amongst them in the work of the ministry." This was November 1726. Subsequently, on February 22, 1727, Edwards was ordained as "a Pastor of the Church of Northampton."

Edwards initially lived with his grandfather, Solomon Stoddard, the longtime pastor. Stoddard had served the Northampton church for more than fifty years and was one of the most successful and influential preachers in New England. He was a serious student of the Scriptures, a widely read author, and a church and community leader. Stoddard's stature throughout the province was so great that he was dubbed the "Congregational Pope" of the Connecticut Valley.[38] Under his vibrant and searching preaching, Northampton experienced five seasons of revival, and the church grew from approximately one hundred communicants in 1677 to nearly five hundred members in 1727, when Edwards arrived.

There is no doubt that Stoddard was a great man and a great minister. Yet his greatness was vitiated by a doctrinal peculiarity that would later haunt his grandson. Although Stoddard answered the call to Northampton in 1669, he preached there for two years without being formally ordained or even becoming a member of the church. Why? The simple reason is that he probably was not converted at the time, and if he had been converted at that time, he lacked assurance as well as any experiential knowledge of Christ. It was not until April 1672, while Stoddard was administering the Lord's Supper, that Christ revealed himself to him.

As a result of his conversion experience, Stoddard developed the erroneous notion that communion, or the Lord's Supper, was a "converting ordinance," that "the place where the soul was likely to receive spiritual light and understanding was at the Lord's table."[39] Previously, Puritan theology was predicated on the assumption that to profess Christ included the profession of actually knowing Christ experientially; however, Stoddard proposed that if individuals understood and professed a faith in the doctrines of Christianity and lived a morally upright life, they should be permitted to partake of the Lord's Supper. Hopefully the so-called halfway Christian would find Christ in the ordinance. "It was better for the church and for the community," Stoddard argued, "that the qualifications required for communion should be as broad as possible."[40]

In effect, an individual with no experiential knowledge of Christ could partake of communion and become a member of the visible church. Thus the sheep gate was opened to wolves. What Edwards thought of this practice when he joined Stoddard as his associate is uncertain. He did acquiesce in it for the time. What we do know, however, is that, years later, when he attempted to tighten the qualifications for communion and membership, the wolves came out of hiding and attacked the shepherd.

Of course, the problems that would later grow from the church's division and the pastor's doctrine were completely out of Edwards's awareness. The distant thunder was hidden by the promising prospect of a long and fruitful ministry. In 1727 he was young, idealistic, and hopeful. He was now in the vocation of his choice and where God had called him.

Moreover, only five months after taking his ministry vows, Edwards took his marriage vows. During his days at Yale, Edwards had met Sarah Pierrepont, the daughter of James Pierrepont, one of the founders of the college, and also a great-granddaughter of Thomas Hooker, founder of Connecticut. She was a young woman with a reputation for uncommon godliness and beauty. Her parents provided her with a "polished education," and "the powers of her mind were of a superior order."[41] When Sarah was only thirteen, twenty-year-old Edwards grew enamored of her profound spirituality and wrote a glowing tribute on the flyleaf of his grammar book:

They say there is a young lady in New Haven who is beloved of that almighty Being, who made and rules the world, and that there are certain seasons in which this great Being, in some way or other invisible, comes to her and fills her mind with exceeding sweet delight, and that she hardly cares for anything, except to meditate on him—that she expects after a while to be received up where he is, to be raised up out of the world and caught up into heaven; being assured that he loves her too well to let her remain at a distance from him always. There she is to dwell with him, and to be ravished with his love and delight forever. Therefore if you present all the world before her, with the richest of its treasures, she disregards it and cares not for it, and is unmindful of any pain of affliction. She has a strange sweetness in her mind, and singular purity in her affections; is most just and conscientious in all her actions; and you could not persuade her to do anything wrong or sinful, if you would give her all the world, lest she should offend this great Being. She is of a wonderful sweetness, calmness and universal benevolence of mind; especially after those seasons in which this great God has manifested himself to her mind. She will sometimes go about from place to place, singing sweetly; and seems to be always full of joy and pleasure; and no one knows for what. She loves to be alone, and to wander in the fields and on the mountains, and seems to have someone invisible always conversing with her.[42]

Unfortunately, we have no record of how Jonathan and Sarah first met, or how their relationship blossomed into marriage. We do know that only four years after penning the above "Apostrophe," Jonathan and Sarah married on July 28, 1727, in New Haven. The young newlyweds then returned to Northampton to establish a new home. The church had set the young minister's salary at one hundred pounds, with another three hundred set aside for the purchase of a homestead. In addition, Edwards received a total of fifty acres of land for pasture and farming. A little over a year later, Sarah gave birth to their first daughter, and the young family was on its way to building a home and a church in Northampton.

Receiving the Mantle

*I*N February 1729, Solomon Stoddard passed away at the age of eighty-one. His mantle fell to Edwards, and the full weight of ministerial responsibilities weighed heavily on the young man's shoulders. Having the duty of preaching three times a week, Edwards rose early and studied hard—so hard in fact that in the spring of 1729 he experienced a second breakdown of his health. In order to recuperate, he spent the summer in New Haven and then East Windsor. He returned to his ministry in late summer, and by all accounts the congregation was pleased with his preaching. "The people of Northampton," his father wrote at the time, "seem to have a great love and respect for him."[43]

It was Edwards's habit as a pastor to socialize little while studying and praying much. According to Samuel Hopkins, Edwards "commonly spent thirteen hours, every day, in his study."[44] Sermon preparation consumed a large part of his time. Like most young preachers, Edwards struggled with the construction of his sermons, striking out a word or phrase and replacing it with a better choice. Sermon construction was hard work. Because he held a high view of the pulpit, he believed it was his duty to thoroughly study the Scriptures and deliver to his congregation the mind of Christ. He once observed, "A minister by his office is to be the guide and instructor of his people. To that end he is to study and search the Scriptures and to teach the people, not the opinions of men—of other divines or of their ancestors—but the mind of Christ. As he is set to enlighten them, so a part of his duty is to rectify their mistakes, and, if he sees them out of the way of truth or duty, to be a voice behind them, saying, 'This is the way, walk ye in it.'"[45]

In the early part of his ministry, Edwards wrote out his sermons in full. The form of his sermons was standard for the time: an exposition of a text, a doctrinal statement or thesis, a development section, and a closing application. When preaching, Edwards relied heavily on his notes. He followed this practice for about twenty years, or until the Great Awakening, when he began to preach from an outline or "skeleton." In contrast to the dramatic itinerant George Whitefield or the explosive orator Samuel Davies, Edwards's style was plain and simple. His voice was low and calm, and he seldom used any gestures, frequently keeping his eyes on his notes or on the bell rope in the back of the church. His great strength as a preacher, however, lay in his clear and forceful argumentation. His logical presentation of biblical truths was nearly irresistible.

The listener's mind was overwhelmed, bowed down by the weight of truth. There was no escaping the force of Edwards's arguments. Moreover, he aimed the arrows of truth at the heart. He spoke in a "pathetic" manner; that is, he preached with a great depth of emotion or earnestness. For Edwards, subjects like heaven, hell, sin, and judgment were living realities, and his own sense of divine things was communicated to his audience. The real key to his success as a preacher, of course, was his intimacy with the Lord. The Spirit of God dwelt in him and flowed through him as he preached.[46]

In addition to sermon preparation, Edwards spent many hours studying Scripture and theology. "Ministers should be diligent in their studies, and in the work of the ministry to which they are called," he said in a sermon on ministerial duty. "And particularly, ministers should be very conversant with the Holy Scriptures; making it very much their business, with the utmost diligence and strictness, to search those holy writings."[47] Edwards heeded his own advice. He studied frequently and recorded his observations in notebooks. These "Miscellanies" eventually equaled nine notebooks with more than fourteen hundred entries from 1722 to the time of his death in 1758. Every insight he thought worth remembering, he jotted in his notebooks. He was so addicted to penning his thoughts that, when riding on horseback, he would often pin a piece of paper to his jacket to recall a significant idea. By the time he arrived at home, he looked as if he were covered with snowflakes. He would then hurry to his study, unpin the scraps, and record his insights.

The initial entries of the miscellanies were chronologically lettered a through z (j and v were omitted). Then he used double letters (aa, bb, . . . zz) and soon after had to start a numerical system. For example:

> **gg.** *Religion. Purpose for Creation.* It is certain that God did not create the world for nothing. It is most certain that if there were no intelligent beings in the world, all the world would be without any good at all. . . . Wherefore, it necessarily follows that intelligent beings are the end of the creation, and that their end must be to behold and admire the doings of God and magnify him for them, and to contemplate his glories in them. Wherefore, religion must be the end of the creation, the great end, the very end.

> **90.** *Christian Religion: None Have Proved It False.* It is a convincing argument for the truth of the Christian religion, and that it stands upon a most sure basis, that none have ever yet been able to prove it false, though there have been many men of all sorts, many fine wits and men of great learning, that have spent themselves and ransacked the world for arguments against it, and this for many ages.[48]

Edwards never intended these notebooks to be published; nevertheless, they are a valuable resource for understanding his theology. His goal was to store up useful material for his pulpit ministry. Biographer Iain Murray commented, "While not directly related to sermon preparation, he saw the entries in his 'Miscellanies' as an integral part of his life and thought both as a Christian and as a minister of the Word of God. . . . Study and writing were not ends in themselves. They were for the service of the gospel."[49]

Edwards understood that, to be effective in the pulpit, he needed to do more than simply master the mechanics of sermon preparation and the techniques of preaching. He also needed something beyond his solid knowledge of the Bible. What Edwards sought in private was communion with God. If he was going to preach effectively—with power—he needed the touch of God. Not content to utter speculative truth alone, he strove to acquire a personal and experiential knowledge of the doctrines he proclaimed. He grasped the simple but profound fact that his inner life was interwoven with his outer work. Ministers should "earnestly seek after much of the spiritual knowledge of Christ, and that they may live in the clear views of his glory. . . . Ministers should be much in seeking God, and conversing with him by prayer, who is the fountain of light and love."[50]

Accordingly, Edwards spent much time in private prayer. He often kept days of fasting and prayer in secret; he commonly spent hours on his knees in prayerful reading of God's Word. His meditation, reading, and writing were all bathed in a spirit of prayer. His study became a holy sanctuary. His prayers were not perfunctory; he earnestly sought genuine, vital communion with God. The power he needed for the pulpit was the power of God.

Yet, more fundamentally, he sought after God because he loved God and yearned for his fellowship. Communion with Christ was his highest joy.

I have sometimes had a sense of the excellent fullness of Christ, and his meetness and suitableness as a Savior; whereby he has appeared to me, far above all, the chief of ten thousands. And his blood and atonement has appeared sweet, and his righteousness sweet; which is always accompanied with an ardency of spirit, and inward strugglings and breathings and groanings, that cannot be uttered, to be emptied of myself, and swallowed up in Christ.[51]

The most important impact of Edwards's closet communion with Christ in the early years of his ministry was a growing sense of personal sinfulness. With God's beauty and holiness serving as a foil, he began to see his sin in a new light, in its true light—the light of God. He was humbled in the dust. Like the prophet Isaiah, gazing on the glory of the thrice-holy God, he cried out, "Woe is me. . . . I am a man of unclean lips." Or like the patriarch Job, when confronted with God's sovereign majesty, he declared, "I have heard of thee by the hearing of the ear: but now mine eye seeth thee. Wherefore I abhor myself, and repent in dust and ashes." Edwards now realized "experientially," not just intellectually, the "exceeding sinfulness of sin."

I have had a vastly greater sense of my own wickedness, and the badness of my heart, than ever I had before my conversion. It has often appeared to me, that if God should mark iniquity against me, I should appear the very worst of all mankind; of all that have been since the beginning of the world to this time; and that I should have by far the lowest place in the world to this time; and that

> I should have by far the lowest place in hell. When others, that have come to talk with me about their soul concerns, have expressed the sense they have had of their own wickedness by saying, that it seemed to them, that they were as bad as the devil himself; I thought their expressions seemed exceeding faint and feeble, to represent my wickedness.[52]

Edwards's experiential knowledge of his own depravity led him to finally submit to, and then champion, the sovereignty of God. Peering into the abyss of his desperately wicked heart, he could fathom no way to salvation except by God's free and sovereign grace.

> And it appears to me, that were it not for free grace, exalted and raised up to the infinite height of all the fullness and glory of the great Jehovah, and the arm of his power and grace stretched forth in all the majesty of his power, and in all the glory of his sovereignty, I should appear sunk down in my sins below hell itself; far beyond the sight of every thing, but the eye of sovereign grace, that can pierce even down to such a depth. And yet, it seems to me that my conviction of sin is exceeding small and faint; it is enough to amaze me, that I have very little sense of my sinfulness. I know certainly, that I have very little sense of my sinfulness. When I have had turns of weeping for my sins, I thought I knew at the time that my repentance was nothing to my sin.[53]

Since Edwards was the pastor of the most prominent church in western Massachusetts, he was asked to give the

"Great and Thursday Lecture" in Boston on July 8, 1731. Reflecting his own spiritual experience, he chose as his text 1 Corinthians 1:29–31: "That no flesh should glory in his presence. But of him are ye in Christ Jesus, who of God is made unto us wisdom, and righteousness, and sanctification, and redemption: that, according as it is written, He that glorieth, let him glory in the Lord." The subject of the sermon was squarely stated: "That God is glorified in the work of redemption in this, that there appears in it so absolute and universal a dependence of the redeemed on him."

"God Glorified in Man's Dependence," as the July 8, 1731, sermon was entitled, was Edwards's first publication. It was also a trumpet call to an apathetic ministry that was straying from the doctrines of the Puritan fathers. A growing number of ministers, such as Benjamin Wadsworth, the president of Harvard, were increasingly latitudinarian.[54] While claiming to be orthodox Calvinists, they were reluctant to scruple over the "finer points" of doctrine. Edwards, on the other hand, courageously "stood before his elders, well aware of the 'enlightened' drift of things, and called them to the faith of their fathers, castigating 'schemes of divinity' that in any way mitigated the doctrine announced in his title."[55] As he said: "Hence those doctrines and schemes of divinity that are in any respect opposite to such an absolute and universal dependence on God, derogate from his glory, and thwart the design of our redemption."[56]

For the next two or three years, Edwards's ministry proceeded normally. His private devotions were augmented by his voracious thirst for knowledge. With pen in hand, he read all the books he could acquire, especially books on divinity. His theology was predominantly Calvinistic, yet "he called no man father."[57] He inherited the Calvinism of his forefathers, yet he was a bold and original thinker who accepted only those doctrines that he believed were most harmonious with the Holy Scriptures. Of course, he studied his Bible above all. For Edwards, "the Bible was supreme: everything was subordinate to the Word of God."[58]

Edwards's pulpit ministry was apparently blessed, since his congregation asked him to publish one of his early (and now most famous) sermons. Entitled *A Divine and Supernatural Light Immediately Imparted to the Soul by the Spirit of God,* Edwards issued a clarion call to personal conversion. Every individual, regardless of his or her relation to the visible church, needed to experience the new birth or regeneration. God imparts to the soul supernatural light or knowledge of Christ and divine things, and this knowledge is saving knowledge. Therefore, "this doctrine may well put us upon examining ourselves, whether we have ever had this divine light let into our souls."[59]

By 1734 there was a "great noise about Arminianism," wrote Edwards, "which seemed to appear with a very threatening aspect upon the interest of religion here."[60] In response, Edwards began to preach on the doctrinal issues in dispute. In a series of sermons collected as *Discourses on Various Important Subjects, Nearly Concerning the Great Affair of the Soul's Eternal Salvation,* Edwards reiterated and defended the traditional doctrine of justification by faith alone, as he had done earlier with the biblical teaching on regeneration.[61]

Several members of his extended family, most notably the Williamses, issued a strong statement to Edwards demanding that he "refrain from the controversy" and "not ... publish his sentiments" regarding it. Edwards refused and was strongly criticized for entering the fray. His cousin Israel Williams had Arminian leanings and attacked him for defending orthodox Reformed theology. Edwards noted: "Great fault was found with 'meddling' with the controversy in the pulpit."[62]

Edwards's refusal to muzzle himself was, according to biographer Sereno Dwight, "an offence not to be forgiven."[63] As we shall see, Israel Williams's lack of forgiveness would fester into a root of bitterness and one day poison the community well.

Breaking Up the Fallow Ground

*A*T THE SAME TIME that Edwards was upholding the banner of Puritan orthodoxy, the Spirit of God swept into his Northampton church. It was Edwards's opinion that the awakening in his church was directly related to his biblical, orthodox preaching. The revival, he said, was "a remarkable testimony of God's approbation of the doctrine of *justification by faith alone.*" As he expounded this doctrine, many were led to question their standing with God and "to engage their hearts in a more earnest pursuit of justification."[64] The result was a general revival in Northampton and several surrounding towns.

In December 1734, several people were "very suddenly" converted. And as the new year dawned, a new interest in the things of Christ was evident throughout Northampton. "A great and earnest concern about the great things of religion and the eternal world, became universal in all parts of the town, and among persons of all degrees, and all ages. . . . Other discourse than of the things of religion would scarcely be tolerated in any company."[65]

According to Edwards, the entire face of the town was wonderfully altered. The old patterns of backbiting and quarreling were put away, the taverns were deserted, family life was renewed, and every day resembled the Sabbath. In addition, the townspeople now earnestly sought the "means of salvation, reading, prayer, meditation, the ordinances of God's house, and private conference." The universal cry was, "What shall I do to be saved?"[66]

By the spring and summer of 1735 the town seemed full of God's presence. Edwards observed, "There were remarkable tokens of God's presence in almost every house." One of the most notable evidences of revival was the spirit of the public worship. He commented, "Our public assemblies were then beautiful: the congregation was alive in God's service, every one earnestly intent on the public worship, every hearer eager to drink in the words of the minister as they came from his mouth; the assembly in general were, from time to time, in tears while the word was preached; some weeping with sorrow and distress, others with joy and love, others with pity and concern for the souls of their neighbors."[67]

Many who had sat under the preaching of both Stoddard and Edwards received a new quickening from the Holy Spirit. The old story of the gospel took on a new beauty and power. Scales fell from their eyes. They beheld the wonders of the cross and the beauties of the Savior. Edwards tells the story of an elderly woman who, having spent many years under Stoddard's powerful ministry, received new spiritual insight during the revival:

> Reading in the New Testament concerning Christ's sufferings for sinners, she seemed to be astonished at what she read, as what was real and very wonderful, but quite new to her. At first, . . . she wondered within herself, that she had never heard of it before; but then immediately recollected herself, and thought she had often heard of it, and read it, but never till now saw it as real. She then cast in her mind how wonderful this was, that the Son of God should undergo such things for sinners, and how she had spent her time in ungratefully sinning against so good a God, and such a Saviour; though she was a person, apparently, of a very blameless and inoffensive life. And she was so overcome by those considerations that her nature was ready to fail under them: those who were about her, and knew not what was the matter, were surprised, and thought she was dying.[68]

Some, whose eyes were suddenly opened, broke into laughter, "tears often at the same time issuing like a flood, and intermingling a loud weeping." Others could not restrain themselves from "crying out with a loud voice, expressing their great admiration." At times some of the people were so overcome with such "longing desires after Christ" that their "natural strength" was taken away. Their bodies weakened, and they seemed to sink under the present sense of the excellency of Christ and the glory of God.[69]

Edwards was convinced that these conversions were genuine, not by the degree of emotional affection or intensity of physical manifestation, but by the godly fruit. First, the new converts had a profound humility. They in no way resembled the "assuming, self-conceited, and self-sufficient airs of enthusiasts." Instead they exhibited a true spirit of meekness and desired to "lie low and in the dust before God." Indeed, they had no greater joy than when they were "lowest in the dust, emptied of themselves, and as it were annihilating themselves before God." Second, they had a love for God's written Word. Edwards wrote, "While God was so remarkably present amongst us by his Spirit, there was no book so delightful as the Bible. . . . There was no time so prized as the Lord's day, and no place in this world so desired as God's house." Third, there was a genuine love for the brethren and for the lost. He noted, "Our converts then remarkably appeared united in dear affection to one another, and many have expressed much of that spirit of love which they have felt toward all mankind; and particularly to those who had been least friendly to them." Perhaps most significantly, Edwards argued that, after the revival receded and the emotions abated, the fruit remained: "We still remain a reformed people, and God has evidently made us a new people." A few may have backslidden, "but in the main, there has been a great and marvellous work of conversion and sanctification among the people here."[70]

It is difficult to say exactly how many people were converted in Northampton during the revival of 1734–35, but Edwards suggests it was nearly three hundred. Of these, there were as many women as men, with the young, middle-aged, and elderly each visited by God.

In the midst of the general rejoicing, however, tragedy struck Edwards. An uncle, Joseph Hawley, committed suicide one Sabbath morning during the height of the revival. Some thought he was driven to despair by the conviction of sin, and therefore Edwards was at least partially responsible. What Hawley's two sons, Joseph Jr. and Elisha, thought of their father's death is unknown, but they continued to sit under Edwards's ministry and received his special care. In reality, Hawley was a victim of hereditary depression, his mother having died the same way. He was not, as we shall see, the last Hawley hounded to self-destruction.

The revival placed new demands on Edwards. Public and private sermons were multiplied, prayer meetings were organized and attended, and personal visitation increased. The quickened townspeople, instead of loitering in the tavern for conversation, were now flocking to the parsonage for counseling. By the autumn of 1735 Edwards was exhausted and his health again failed him. Since it was then believed that horse riding built up one's physical constitution, Edwards journeyed to New York and New Jersey. During the trip he reestablished ties with several men who would later labor with him in the Great Awakening: Ebenezer Pemberton was pastor of the Wall Street Church in New York, Jonathan Dickinson had settled in Elizabeth Town, and John Pierson was laboring in the parish of Woodbridge.

While visiting Jersey, Edwards providentially met the Tennent brothers, who also were to play a major role in the upcoming revival. Their father, William Tennent, was a Presbyterian pastor and a teacher at his "Log College" just north of Philadelphia. Each of his four sons—Gilbert, William Jr., John, and Charles—were preachers of "revitalized" Christianity. Although John died in 1732, the other brothers reported to Edwards that, like Northampton, their parishes had experienced recent awakenings. This was the first he had heard of any revival outside Northampton. He later learned that the revival touched many of the churches in the Connecticut Valley as well: South-Hadley, Deerfield, Hatfield, Enfield, East Windsor (his father's parish), Coventry, New Haven, and elsewhere.[71] Each of the men he visited had seen the power of God visit his ministry in the conversion of souls. Yet their desire for greater revival only intensified with their success.

When Edwards returned to Northampton, the congregation had voted (by a narrow margin) to construct a new meetinghouse. Work proceeded slowly throughout 1736. By June 1737 the spire was finished, and on December 25, 1737, the new building was occupied. Unfortunately, the building project was less than a harmonious effort: it led to a recurrence of Northampton's besetting sin of contention. In May 1737, Edwards reproved his people for their contentious spirit: "I suppose for these thirty years people have not known how to manage scarcely any public business without dividing into parties . . . of late, time after time that old party spirit has appeared again, and particularly this spring."[72]

Edwards realized that although the work of the recent revival was real, it was not necessarily deep. Conversion is not consecration. These new converts might be genuinely saved, but now they needed to be genuinely sanctified. Thus he spent the next two years preaching on holiness and Christian growth. In both *Charity and Its Fruits* (1738) and *A History of the Work of Redemption* (1739), he drove home the message dear to his own heart: "He that truly loves God, constantly seeks after God in the course of his life: seeks his grace, and acceptance, and glory." In light of God's gracious visitation of Northampton, with the many conversions that resulted, Edwards pleaded with his people to respond with a "holy, serious, just, humble, charitable" devotion of themselves to God and one another.[73]

Increased demands on Edwards's time notwithstanding, he did not neglect his wife and family. He daily met with Sarah in his study for prayer and encouragement as well as planning family business. Many of the daily concerns of the household, such as organizing chores, buying food, and governing the children, were placed in her hands. By 1738, the Edwardses had six children. Daughter Sarah was born in 1728, and the rest followed, with one every two years: Jerusha (1730), Esther (1732), Mary (1734), Lucy (1736), and Timothy (1738). It was Edwards's habit to conduct family prayers both in the morning and before bedtime. Often he would take his children into his study individually and address them concerning their spiritual condition. He also taught his children spiritual truth by catechizing them in the Westminster Shorter Catechism on the evening before every Sabbath.

In the meantime, word of the "frontier" revival was spreading. There was a great deal of interest and not a little skepticism concerning the reports of Northampton. Responding to questions from Benjamin Coleman, a prominent Boston pastor, Edwards had earlier (in May

1735) given a written report of the awakening. Coleman, in turn, had passed on Edwards's reply to two English divines, John Guyse and Isaac Watts, who wrote back asking for a more detailed report. Edwards complied with their request and dispatched a large letter (on November 6, 1736) in which he estimated the number of converts at Northampton and also mentioned that the revival was occurring in isolated churches throughout New England. Elisha Williams had also written to Watts in May 1736, stating that "there has been a remarkable revival of religion in several parts of this country, in ten parishes in the county of Hampshire, in the Massachusetts province, where it first began a little more than a year since, and in near twenty parishes of this colony [Connecticut]."[74]

When Guyse and Watts received Edwards's letter, they were so impressed with the report that they immediately decided to publish it. "So strange and surprising work of God that we have not heard anything like it since the Reformation . . . should be published and left upon record," they wrote to Coleman. Eventually, in the autumn of 1737, Edwards's letter was published in London with the lengthy title *A Faithful Narrative of the Surprising Work of God in the Conversion of Many Souls in Northampton, and Neighboring Towns and Villages of New Hampshire, in New England.*[75]

This little book with the long title became, through God's providence, one of the most popular and influential publications of its day. In only two years *Faithful Narrative* went through three editions and twenty printings and reached the far corners of the colonies and Britain. Church historian Sydney E. Ahlstrom noted, "Far away in

Boston, and farther still in England and Scotland, prominent theologians and ministers were thrilled by the news and convinced that a new day of the Lord was at hand."[76] John Wesley, for instance, notes in his journal: "I set out for Oxford. In walking I read the truly surprising narrative of the conversions lately wrought in and about the town of Northampton, in New England. Surely 'this is the Lord's doing, and it is marvellous in our eyes.'"[77] Reading about the works of God in Northampton, Wesley and others were inspired to believe that God could in their own day bring in a similar harvest of souls. They were, in effect, led to desire and pray for a great awakening.

WHITEFIELD AND THE GREAT AWAKENING

*T*HE GRAND REVIVAL KNOWN as the Great Awakening shook the English-speaking world during the late 1730s and the 1740s. The flames of revival that scorched the American colonies were likewise ablaze in England, Scotland, and Ireland. Yet the very notion of "revival" supposes a previous state of "decline," or at least complacency, in religious and spiritual matters. If the late '30s and the '40s were a time of revival, what conditions characterized the state of Western religion before this time?

In England, Deism had the upper hand in religious circles. As an expression of religious rationalism, Deism advocated that God was little more than a First Cause, a force that made the world the way a clock maker constructs a clock. Then, having set the mechanism in motion, he simply allowed it to run according to natural laws. This deity, therefore, did not interfere with his own laws; thus miraculous intervention by God was excluded. Under the name of "natural religion," authors such as Matthew Tindal, John Toland, and Thomas Woolston claimed that Deism was true primitive Christianity.

Of course, Deism did not go unchallenged by the established church: Bishop Joseph Butler wrote his masterful apologetic *The Analogy of Revealed Religion,* and William Law penned *An Appeal to All That Doubt the Truths of Revelation.* The famous hymnist Isaac Watts, who took an avid interest in the revival in Northampton, also wielded his sword in the Trinitarian controversy when he issued his sublime *A Treatise on the Trinity.* Nevertheless, British Christianity proved itself to be little more than a sedate and timid religious ethic unable to resist the decay of spirituality and morality. Mourning the lack of spiritual power among both the clergy and people, Rev. [John] Howe noted, "It is plain, too sadly plain, there is a great retraction of the Spirit of God even from us [ministers]. We know not how to speak living sense unto souls; how to get within you: our words die in our mouths, or drop and die between you and us. We even faint when we speak; long-experienced unsuccessfulness makes us despond: we speak not as persons that hope to prevail, that expect to make you serious, heavenly, mindful of God, and to walk more like Christians."[78]

Amid this deistical decline in religion, George Whitefield was brought into the world. Since he played such a large role in the Great Awakening, a few words about his history are in order. Born in December 1714, Whitefield entered college at eighteen and met the Wesley brothers a year later. He was ordained at the age of twenty-one on Trinity Sunday, 1736. Shortly thereafter, he was invited to minister in London, and while there he first received letters from friends in Georgia, bidding him to come to the colony and help them. After being detained sometime in London, Whitefield left England in January 1738 and arrived in Savannah in May of the same year. While there, he observed the deplorable conditions of some orphan children. Possibly at the suggestion of Charles Wesley, he determined to build an orphanage. To raise funds, he returned to England in early December.

A week later, on a Sunday, December 21, Whitefield preached and solicited funds for his orphanage. Within a matter of days, however, the established clergy took issue with his doctrine of regeneration and viciously attacked him from their pulpits and in the press. Having the church doors slammed in his face, Whitefield marched to the fields. On Wednesday, February 21, he preached his first open-air sermon at Kingswood, with nearly two thousand attending. On Friday, he preached to about four or five thousand, and on Sunday to approximately ten thousand. The Great Awakening had erupted!

But Whitefield had not forgotten his orphans. His goal was to return to Savannah and build them a home. So he entrusted the blossoming revival in England to the Wesleys and sailed to the colonies.

At the time of his arrival on October 30, 1739, a number of locations (Northampton among them) were already experiencing revival of their own. Prior to 1720, however, the spiritual and religious conditions in America were little better than in England. Due to the influence of the Half-Way Covenant and Stoddard's doctrine of the Lord's Supper, many unconverted people became members of the visible church. Worse still, many unconverted men had entered the ministry. Thus, "the difference between the church and the world was vanishing away. Church discipline was neglected, and the growing laxness of morals was invading the churches."[79]

In the 1720s things began to change, however. For the next fifteen years, evangelical revivals were experienced in different parts of the colonies. In Pennsylvania, for instance, Germans of many denominations—Lutheran, Mennonite, Quaker—had settled northwest of Philadelphia in a community known as Germantown. During this period, old pietistic influences were rekindled, especially among the Mennonites and Baptists. In New Jersey, the ministry of Theodorus Frelinghuysen, a Dutch Reformed minister, began to bear fruit in the Raritan Valley. In the middle colonies, Presbyterians also experienced awakenings through the efforts of William Tennent and his sons. And in New England, of course, there was Edwards. So by the time Whitefield arrived in Pennsylvania in 1739, the colonial soil had been plowed and was awaiting the sower and his seed.

Whitefield made four tours of the colonies between 1738 and 1740. The first, or Winter Tour, began in Pennsylvania in November 1739 and covered New Jersey, New York, Maryland, Virginia, and North and South Carolina. During this tour, Whitefield made two important acquaintances, those of Gilbert Tennent and Benjamin Franklin—the latter became his publisher in America. In

January, the tour ended at Savannah, the site where the orphanage was to be built.

The Spring Tour, which began in April 1740, again took Whitefield to Philadelphia and New York. After four and a half weeks of travel he returned to Georgia on June 5, "having accomplished the purposes for which he had taken the tour, for not only had he been mightily used of God in the reviving of the work in the Middle Colonies, but had collected about 500 pounds with which to continue the House of Mercy in Georgia."[80]

The Summer Tour, which lasted the greater part of July 1740 and covered Charleston and the surrounding area, was fruitful; although it was marked by tremendous opposition from Commissary Alexander Garden of Charleston.

Whitefield's final and most extensive tour was in the autumn of 1740. Having arrived in Rhode Island on Sunday, September 14, he spent the next four months traveling throughout New England. Not only did he meet with Edwards in Northampton, he also preached from his pulpit. Moreover, during the Autumn Tour, Whitefield had a great influence on Jonathan Belcher, the governor of Massachusetts. In 1745, Belcher became governor of New Jersey, and in 1746 he played a key role in the establishment of a new Presbyterian theological school—Princeton College.

The effect of Whitefield's preaching was nothing short of dramatic. For example, an unsigned letter to the *New England Journal* stated: "I went to hear him in the evening at the Presbyterian Church. . . . I never in my life saw so attentive an audience. Mr. Whitefield spoke as one having authority: all he said was Demonstration, Life and Power. The people's eyes and ears hung on his lips. They greedily devoured every word. I came home astonished. Every scruple vanished; I never saw or heard the like; and I said within myself, Surely God is with this man of a truth!"[81]

When Whitefield was in Philadelphia, Benjamin Franklin heard him preach and gave striking testimony to his persuasive powers. In reference to Whitefield's pleading for the Georgia orphans, Franklin stated:

> Mr. Whitefield . . . preached up this charity, and made large collections, for his eloquence had a wonderful power over the hearts and purses of his hearers, of which I myself was an instance.
>
> I happened . . . to attend one of his sermons, in the course of which I perceived he intended to finish with a collection, and I silently resolved he should get nothing from me. I had in my pocket a handful of copper money, three or four silver dollars, and five pistoles in gold. As he proceeded I began to soften, and concluded to give the coppers. Another stroke of his oratory made me ashamed of that, and determined me to give the silver; and he finished so admirably that I emptied my pocket wholly into the collector's dish, gold and all.[82]

Everywhere that Whitefield went, his preaching had a powerful impact. His *Journal* records that "many men melted into tears" and that many began to press upon him in his private hours. On Thursday, April 17, during the Spring Tour, he stated that he "preached to upwards of ten thousand people. . . . Hundreds were graciously melted." Two days later, he recorded "giving answers and praying with divers persons who applied to me under deep convictions."[83] In summing up the Spring Tour, he declared, "Religion is all the talk; and I think I can say, the Lord Jesus hath gotten Himself the victory in many hearts."[84]

By the time Whitefield arrived at Northampton in 1740, the revival had already been under way for months. According to Edwards, in the spring of that year, there was a "visible alteration" in the town. People were more serious and religious in their conversation, and many began to consult Edwards concerning their spiritual condition.

On October 17, Whitefield crossed the ferry to Northampton and preached four sermons at the church and one at Edwards's home in the space of three days. Referring to the church services, Whitefield wrote: "Preached this morning and good Mr. Edwards wept during the whole time of exercise. The people were equally affected; and in the afternoon, the power increased yet more. I have not seen four such gracious meetings together since my arrival."[85] Edwards concurred: "The congregation was extraordinarily melted by every sermon; almost the whole assembly being in tears for a great part of sermon time."[86]

Edwards and his guest then set out for East Windsor, where Whitefield preached on October 21. The next day the two parted company. Edwards headed up the Connecticut River, and Whitefield finished up his tour of New England. In the meantime, the revival in Northampton increased throughout 1740. Edwards noted:

> The revival at first appeared chiefly among professors and those that had entertained hope that they were in a state of salvation, to whom Mr. Whitefield chiefly addressed

> himself; but in a very short time there appeared an awak-
> ening and deep concern among some young persons, that
> looked upon themselves in a Christless state; and there
> were some hopeful appearances of conversion, and some
> professors were greatly revived. In about a month or six
> weeks, there was a great attention in the town, both as to
> the revival of professors and the awakening of others.[87]

The revival gathered steam during the last part of the year, with a powerful work occurring among Northampton's young people. By December, "religious subjects almost wholly took up the conversation" of the town's youth.

The quickening spread during the winter and spring. In May 1741, Edwards preached in a private house. Toward the end of his message, several people were so overcome with the "glory of divine things" that there was "a very visible effect upon their bodies." The young people present were quickly moved into another room, and after a short time of discussion with Edwards, they were "overcome with distress" about their sinful condition. The room filled with "outcries, faintings and the like." The awakening of the young was so extensive that Edwards thereafter set up special meetings for them where he would give "counsels proper to their age." It was not uncommon at these meetings for the room to be "filled with cries," and when the children were dismissed, "they almost all of them went home crying aloud through the streets."[88]

As the Great Awakening gained momentum, Edwards was often called upon to preach at churches outside Northampton. In July 1741, for instance, Edwards and

Eleazer Wheelock went to Enfield, where Edwards gave
his famous sermon "Sinners in the Hands of an Angry
God."

Wheelock thought the people of Enfield were "loose
and vain," not having been touched by the revival. On
the evening of July 8, at an unannounced lecture, Edwards entered the pulpit and declared his text, Deuteron-
omy 32:35: "Their foot shall slide in due time." His
doctrine, he warned the congregation, was that "there is
nothing that keeps wicked men, at any one moment, out
of hell, but the mere pleasure of God." There is no lack of
power in God to send every sinner to hell immediately if
he should choose to do so. Indeed, since wicked men
justly deserve damnation, and even now are under God's
righteous wrath, nothing but God's mere pleasure keeps
them from descending into hell at any given instant.
God's arm is not shortened. Thus, there is no security for
the wicked. God can take sinners out of this world in
countless ways. "Unconverted men walk over the pit of
hell on a rotten covering, and there are innumerable
places in this covering so weak that they won't bear their
weight, and these places are not seen. The arrows of
death fly unseen at noonday; the sharpest sight can't discern them." The dreadful reality of unregenerate men is
that they "are held in the hand of God over the pit of hell;
they deserved the fiery pit, and are already sentenced to
it. . . . The devil is waiting for them, hell is gaping for
them, the flames gather and flash about them, and would
fain lay hold on them, and swallow them up." Only the
"mere arbitrary will" of an incensed God keeps them
from eternal destruction.

With holy zeal in his eyes, Edwards bore down on the carnally secure: "The bow of God's wrath is bent, and the arrow made ready on the string, and justice bends the arrow at your heart, and strains the bow, and it is nothing but the mere pleasure of God, and that of an angry God . . . that keeps the arrow one moment from being made drunk with your blood." Do not be deceived by false cries of "peace and safety." Your condition is as precarious as a spider hung over a fire. "The God that holds you over the pit of hell, much as one holds a spider, or some loathsome insect, over the fire, abhors you, and is dreadfully provoked; his wrath towards you burns like fire; he looks upon you as worthy of nothing else, but to be cast into the fire." Edwards then pleaded with his audience to ponder their perilous exposure to punishment:

> O Sinners! Consider the fearful danger you are in: 'tis a great furnace of wrath, a wide and bottomless pit, full of the fire of wrath, that you are held over in the hand of that God, whose wrath is provoked and incensed as much against you as against any of the damned in hell: you hang by a slender thread, with the flames of divine wrath flashing about it, and ready every moment to singe it, and burn it asunder; and you have no interest in any mediator, and nothing to lay hold of to save yourself, nothing to keep off the flames of wrath, nothing of your own, nothing that you ever have done, nothing that you can do, to induce God to spare you one moment.[89]

As the horrible reality set in, there was a great groaning throughout the meeting place. Numbers began to shriek and cry out, "What shall I do to be saved?" Others howled, "Oh, I am going to hell!"[90] Some clung to their seats for fear of falling at that very moment into the burning lake of fire. Edwards paused and tried to restrain the groans and weeping. He then continued: "Now God stands ready to pity you; this is a day of mercy; you may cry now with some encouragement of obtaining mercy: but when once the day of mercy is past, your most lamentable and dolorous cries and shrieks will be in vain." Echoing the words of the angels at Sodom, Edwards admonished all to flee from the wrath to come: "Haste and escape for your lives, look not behind you, escape to the mountain, lest you be consumed."[91]

Wheelock, observing the scene, said the people were "bowed down with an awful conviction of their sin and danger." After Edwards descended the pulpit, the people were gathered into groups for prayer. Many were changed. As another eyewitness recorded: "Several souls were hopefully wrought upon that night, and oh the cheerfulness and pleasantness of their countenances that received comfort."[92]

Incidents like this were common throughout the Great Awakening. In fact, such manifestations as jerking, fainting, and crying out occurred during the spring and summer of 1741 in Northampton. Edwards commented: "It was a very frequent thing to see a house full of outcries, faintings, convulsions, and such like, both with distress, and also with admiration and joy." In some cases, individuals were "so affected, and their bodies so overcome, that they could not go home, but were obliged to stay all night where they were."[93]

As might be expected, these extreme manifestations caused some onlookers to doubt the authenticity of the revival. Did an extraordinary show of affection signal an exceptional work of grace? Was this God, the devil, or the flesh? How could one tell?

Similar questions were on many minds when Edwards was asked to give the commencement sermon at Yale in September 1741. His message, titled "The Distinguishing Marks of a Work of the Spirit of God," was Edwards's answer to these questions. He chose as his text 1 John 4:1: "Beloved, believe not every spirit, but try the spirits whether they are of God: because many false prophets are gone out into the world." In a highly rational but not dispassionate presentation, Edwards argued that the Great Awakening should not be discounted because of the extreme physical manifestations such as "tears, trembling, groans, loud outcries, agonies of body, or the failing of bodily strength." On the other hand, neither do these physical symptoms prove that the work is truly of God. "A work is not to be judged of by any effects on the bodies of men; such as tears, trembling, groans, loud outcries, agonies of body, or the failing of bodily strength. The influence persons are under is not to be judged of one way or other by such effects on the body; and the reason is because the Scripture nowhere gives us any such rule."[94] So how do we judge?

We "try the spirits" or judge a particular work by the rules set forth in the written Word of God. That is the standard by which we judge all subjective experience or physical manifestations. And according to Edwards, there were five "distinguishing marks" of a true work of God's

Spirit. The Holy Spirit always (1) engenders a greater esteem of Jesus; (2) operates against the kingdom of Satan; (3) causes men to have a "greater regard to the Holy Scriptures"; (4) leads people into truth; and (5) operates as a spirit of love to God and man. If these marks are present, despite irregularities, then one can be sure that the Spirit of God is at work.[95]

Edwards realized that the awakening was tainted in some cases by fanaticism and error. These "stumbling blocks," as he called them, were not likely to be removed; rather, they might even increase. Yet instead of sitting back as cool spectators, it was the duty of all Christians, and especially Christian ministers, to do all in their power to promote the revival. Edwards then issued this strong admonition: "Let us all be warned, by no means to oppose, or do any thing in the least to clog or hinder the work; but, on the contrary, do our utmost to promote it."[96]

By publishing this sermon, Edwards became the awakening's leading proponent. He was now marked as New England's principal defender of revival.

In Defense of Revival

*T*HE AWAKENING CONTINUED UNABATED during the winter of 1741–42. And for his part, Edwards was doing his "utmost" to promote the revival. Besides his labors at Northampton, he frequently journeyed to preach in other parishes, leaving his pulpit in the hands of visiting ministers. On one occasion in late January 1742, Edwards traveled to Leicester on a "missionary tour" and turned his pulpit over to Samuel Buell. Under Buell's preaching the excitement in Northampton reached a feverish pitch. Services were conducted nearly every night for two weeks, and when outside the pulpit, Buell was frantic in private ministry.

Around this time Sarah Edwards experienced a marvelous quickening from God. "I felt more perfectly subdued and weaned from the world," she later wrote, "than I had ever been conscious of before. . . . I was entirely swallowed up in God, as my only portion, and his honour and glory was the object of my supreme delight." Throughout the night of January 28, Sarah tasted the blessedness of her dear Savior. "All night I continued in a constant, clear, and lively sense of the heavenly sweetness of Christ's excellent and transcendent love." This constant calmness of soul was like a "flowing and reflowing of heavenly and divine love, from Christ's heart to mine." There was no earthly pleasure that could compare to the "pure delight which fed and satisfied the soul." It was "a sweetness which my soul was lost in. It seemed to be all that my feeble frame could sustain, of that fullness of joy which is felt by those who behold the face of Christ, and share his love in the heavenly world."[97]

Sarah's experience bespeaks all that was good in the revival. But a darker expression of the revival was beginning to surface in Northampton. When Edwards returned home, he found the town in "a great and continual commotion" and in "very extraordinary circumstances." New, suspicious manifestations were emerging: "There were some instances of persons lying in a sort of trance, remaining perhaps for a whole twenty-four hours motionless, and with their senses locked up; but in the meantime under strong imaginations, as though they went to heaven and had there a vision of glorious and delightful objects."[98]

What did Edwards think of these extreme displays? He denounced them in no uncertain terms. They were instigated by the devil. "When the people were raised to this height, Satan took the advantage."[99] Edwards noted that the early part of the revival had been very pure, "having less of a corrupt mixture than in the former great outpouring of the Spirit in 1735 and 1736." Yet in the latter part of the Great Awakening (1742), his people were "infected from abroad"—by which he probably meant Buell and some of his devotees who had followed him from Suffield to Northampton. Their raptures, violent emotions, and vehement zeal beguiled some of Edwards's flock into imagining they were superior in grace. This was a "strange influence," thought Edwards. And he labored with difficulty to deliver some from their delusion.[100]

Reflecting later on events in Northampton, Edwards was convinced more than ever for the need to "try the spirits." Physical manifestations alone tell us nothing about the nature of a person's spiritual experience. Extreme emotions or bodily manifestations, in and of themselves, are not a sure sign of God's gracious work. Rather, the spirit must be judged by its long-term fruit. It is not enough for the emotions to be elevated or the body agitated; the soul itself must be touched and transformed. As Edwards put it, we must look to "the temper of the soul" not only at the time of quickening but "remaining afterwards."[101] Or, as Christ said: "By their fruits ye shall know them."

Indeed, if there was ever a time when discernment yielded a premium, it was during the latter days of the Great Awakening. As it turned out, the same aberrations happening at Northampton were transpiring elsewhere, among both laity and clergy.

One of the most notorious examples of "enthusiasm," as it was called, was the Rev. James Davenport, the "arch-fanatic" of the Great Awakening.[102] Davenport was born at Stamford, Connecticut, a great-grandson of New Haven founder John Davenport and a graduate of Yale. Since 1738 he had been pastor of the old Puritan church at Southold on Long Island. Being much impressed with the itinerant ministry of Whitefield and the Tennents, Davenport fancied he was called to imitate them. Claiming that he had received a "word" from God to "go into the Philistine's camp," he deserted his church and began to travel to other churches uninvited. Under his preaching there probably were a number of conversions; however, there was also an increase of bizarre manifestations: jerkings, faintings, and trances. He encouraged such behavior by his own eccentricity. An eyewitness wrote:

> He has no knack at raising the Passions, but by a violent straining of his Lungs, and the most extravagant wreathings of his Body, which at the same Time that it creates Laughter and Indignation in most, occasions great meltings, screamings, crying, swooning, and Fits in some others. . . . Were you to see him in his most violent agitations, you would be apt to think, that he was a Madman just broke from his Chains: But especially had you seen him returning from the Common Way thro' the Streets, he with his Hands extended, his Head thrown back, and his Eyes staring up to Heaven, attended with so much Disorder, that they look'd more like a Company of Bacchanalians after a mad Frolick, than sober Christians who had been worshipping God.[103]

Davenport would often show up at a church, demand the pulpit, and if refused, denounce the minister as unconverted. His fanatical harangues against the clergy aroused resentment everywhere he went. And since he believed most ministers were unconverted, he exhorted their flocks to desert them. Thus he was a major source of alienation and bitter division.

It is not surprising, then, that the civil and ecclesiastical authorities banded together to resist him. In 1742, he was arrested in Connecticut for violating the law against itinerant preaching, adjudged mentally disturbed, and deported to Long Island. But filled with the "spirit of martyrdom," Davenport headed for Boston, where he again filled the streets with denunciatory preaching and extravagant claims of divine "impressions." A convention of ministers there denounced Davenport for his "errors, irregularities, and mischiefs" and warned the people that he was "deeply tinctured with a spirit of enthusiasm."[104] A few weeks later he was arrested, declared non compos mentis, and expelled.

Davenport's fanatical finale took place in March 1743, when he gathered a group of zealots in New London to start a new church. In response to divine dreams, he told his followers that they needed to purify themselves from worldliness; accordingly, "he ordered wigs, cloakes and breeches, hoods, gowns, rings, jewels and necklaces to be brought together into his room, and laid in a heap, that they might, by his solemn decree, be committed to the flames."[105] He next issued a list of books that likewise needed to burned—evangelical heroes such as John Flavel, Benjamin Colman, Increase Mather, and others. On March 6, Davenport and his followers marched to the wharf, and in a frenzied ceremony burned the collected articles while shouting "Hallelujah" and "Glory to God."[106]

The outlandish behavior of Davenport and others gave ammunition to the enemies of the awakening. As early as January 1742 an anonymous author published "The Wonderful Narrative," which was a pseudo-history of the "French Prophets, Their Agitations, Extasies and Imaginations." The design of the author (probably Charles Chauncy, junior pastor of Boston's First Church) was to blacken the revival with the label of "fanaticism." Chauncy's intention was to discredit the revival by showing that such actions as fainting or outcries were not signs of the Holy Spirit but the work of enthusiasm or even imposture, as was the case with the French Prophets.[107] Next, in August of the same year, another "Letter" (again probably by Chauncy) appeared in which the writer vilified the ministry of Whitefield. "I freely acknowledge, wherever he went he generally moved the passions, especially of the younger people, and the females among them. . . . But so far as I could judge . . . the town, in general, was not mended in those things wherein a reformation was greatly needed." This testimony, though, is directly contradicted by the statement of Benjamin Franklin, hardly a "friend" of the revival. Chauncy continued his letter with a denunciation of the revival as nothing more than a "Spirit of Superstition and Enthusiasm reigning in the Land."[108]

Edwards entered the fray in March 1743 (providentially the same month that Davenport conducted his flaming farewell service) by publishing *Some Thoughts Concerning the Present Revival.* Chauncy's reply, *Seasonable Thoughts on the State of Religion in New-England,* was circulating six months later. It was clear that the battle lines were now drawn, with the troops gathering around Edwards and Chauncy as their opposing generals.

Chauncy's position was that the "revival" (if it could be called that) may have done some good, but on the whole there was more evil than good, and therefore the "commotion" should stop. In particular, Chauncy and other anti-revivalists criticized not only the bodily manifestations apparent in the revival, but also itinerant preaching, lay exhorting, censoriousness, church separations, and other miscellaneous doctrinal errors such as the belief in direct divine impressions.

In *Some Thoughts,* Edwards had to walk a tightrope: he had to defend the revival from its critics but also guard the revival from its friends. (With "friends" like Davenport, this was no easy task!)

Edwards believed that, in the main, the revival was a veritable work of God's Spirit. This is apparent from the amount of space he gives to defending and promoting the revival. In fact, in the early Edinburgh edition of *Some Thoughts* (1743), Edwards devotes fifty pages to arguing that the revival is indeed "a glorious work of God." He then devotes section 2 of the work to exhorting all to "acknowledge this work" (twenty-four pages), and section 3 provides advice for "what ought to be done to promote this work" (thirty-one pages). Clearly, Edwards believed the revival was genuine and deserved the active support of all Christians.[109]

Nevertheless, he now realized that the revival had been infected with carnal enthusiasm and demonic influence. Therefore, he devoted the largest section of *Some Thoughts* to "things to be corrected and avoided." Here he addressed the "friends" of the revival who, through errors and extremes, were bringing the revival into disfavor. In agreement with the anti-revivalists, Edwards castigated fanatics for spiritual pride, for denouncing ministers, for separating from their churches, for following immediate revelations, and for other faults.[110] Despite these defects, Edwards still maintained that the awakening was a true work of God.

Meanwhile, as *Some Thoughts* was circulating throughout Great Britain and the colonies, Edwards was back in Northampton, managing the awakening there. Perhaps in response to some of the excesses, he decided to lead his people in a solemn public covenant with God. On March 16, 1742, the people of God at Northampton swore: "We do this day present ourselves before the Lord, to renounce our evil ways, we put away our abominations from before God's eyes, and with one accord, to renew our engagements to seek and serve God." As the covenant stipulated, the people promised to observe the rules of honesty, justice, and uprightness; to not injure their neighbors; to provide restitution for past wrongs; to refrain from backbiting and strife; to not violate justice for private gain; to not indulge ill will or hold secret grudges; to do nothing that might gratify lust and hinder the spirit of religion; and to fulfill all the relative duties of parents, spouses, and children. Finally, the people promised "to be often strictly examining ourselves by these promises, especially before the sacrament of the Lord's supper; and beg of God that he would, for Christ's sake, keep us from wickedly dissembling in these our solemn vows."[111]

This covenant was essentially a formal expression of

Edwards's belief about real spiritual experience: it must always produce a greater dedication to God and man. In a way, the public covenant was a test for all those in his church who believed they had been quickened during the revival. Would they step forward and publicly dedicate themselves to God?

Edwards also took further steps to see that his flock understood the true nature of saving and sanctifying grace. Throughout late 1742 and 1743 he preached a series of sermons on 1 Peter 1:18, which were later published (1746) as *A Treatise Concerning the Religious Affections.* Today hailed as a masterpiece of "religious psychology," *Religious Affections* was Edwards's attempt to get at the root issue in the controversy over the Great Awakening: namely, what is the nature of true conversion? Or as Edwards expressed it: "What is the nature of true religion? And wherein do lie the distinguishing notes of that virtue and holiness that is acceptable in the sight of God?"[112]

The purpose of the *Religious Affections* was to aid converts of the revival in evaluating their own condition. The "distinguishing notes" or "signs" of true conversion were not infallible marks for separating the sheep from the goats, for only God truly knows the hearts of men, but rather tools for self-examination. He wrote:

> Though it is plain that Christ has given rules to all Christians to enable them to judge of professors of religion whom they are concerned with, so far as is necessary for their own safety, and to prevent their being led into a snare by false teachers and false pretenders to religion; and though it be also beyond doubt that the Scriptures do

abound with rules which may be very serviceable to ministers, in counselling and conducting souls committed to
their care in things appertaining to their spiritual and eternal state; yet it is also evident, that it was never God's design to give us any rules by which we may *certainly* know
who of our fellow professors are His, and to make a *full
and clear* separation between sheep and goats.[113]

This caveat was needful; for in a few short years Edwards would be accused of doing this very thing.

CONTROVERSY AND DISMISSAL

*B*Y 1743 THE GREAT Awakening in New England had come to a halt. And a year later trouble was stirring in Northampton. In fact, several events coincided to make 1744 a significant year in Edwards's story.

The first sign of trouble was the "bad book case," as it has come to be called. In March 1744, Edwards was informed that a handbook on midwifery was being circulated among some young people. Some boys (or young men) were viewing the diagrams, joking obscenely, and teasing some of the town's girls. When Edwards learned of the situation, he called a church meeting and asked a committee to assist him in investigating the matter. The church agreed. But after the committee was established and a hearing time was set, Edwards read a list of names of those he wanted present. Some of the leading mem-

bers' children were named. The parents were shocked—
and offended. But Edwards blundered; he did not clarify
that some of the youth mentioned were being summoned
only as witnesses, not as suspects. According to Sereno
Dwight, "The town was suddenly all in a blaze." After
two months of intense commotion, two young men,
Simeon and Timothy Root, confessed before the church.
But the damage was done. Writing many years later,
Dwight commented that, after this incident, Edwards
"greatly lost his influence" in Northampton. There was
"no great visible success" in his ministry in subsequent
years.[114]

The alienation caused by the bad book case was evident in Edwards's battle with the church over his salary.
Due to the depreciation of Massachusetts currency, he
had been underpaid for several years. But when he asked
for a raise in 1744, he was stonewalled. It was not until
1748 that his pay was increased. Yet in the course of the
dispute, the relationship between pastor and people deteriorated.

The third problem that developed was theological. As
was seen earlier, Solomon Stoddard had taught that an unregenerate person could partake of the Lord's Supper provided that he made a profession of faith and avoided
flagrant sin. A testimony of a salvation experience was not
necessary. As a result the visible church became a mixed
multitude. By 1744 Edwards had come to a position on
communion that differed from Stoddard's and hence,
from the long-standing practice of Northampton. As we
shall see, this difference of opinion would be used later as
a pretext for dismissing Edwards as pastor.

In the midst of these conflicts and his many duties as pastor, preacher, and revivalist, Edwards was heartened by close family relationships. His early love and admiration for his wife, Sarah, never abated. She was his perfect help-meet. She governed the home in his many absences, orchestrated the chores while he studied, and graciously entertained guests who came to confer or study with her husband. One such guest was Samuel Hopkins, who visited the Northampton parsonage in the winter of 1741, when the Great Awakening was at its height, and resided there for seven months. As an eyewitness to the Edwardses' relationship, Hopkins noted the "great harmony and mutual love and esteem" that sustained husband and wife.[115]

Hopkins also saw how the children were trained and disciplined. In addition to the six children already mentioned, Edwards and Sarah were to have five more: Susannah (1740), Eunice (1743), Jonathan (1745), Elizabeth (1747), and Pierrepont (1750). With eleven children in the home, order was a virtue, and the children had to strictly observe a curfew of nine o'clock. "The hour of retirement was firmly kept," wrote Hopkins. Even the older daughters were required to comply; visiting suitors were dismissed by the chime. Nothing was permitted to "intrude on the religion and order of the family."[116] Both parents rarely resorted to corporal punishment. Edwards disciplined his children "with the greatest calmness and commonly without striking a blow." Sarah was equally successful in the exercise of her authority. She taught the children to "obey her cheerfully, without loud, angry words, much less heavy blows."[117]

As with any family, of course, the Edwards children were not "little angels." The eldest daughter, Sarah, for instance, had a quick temper. And according to an old tradition, when Elihu Parsons came to Edwards asking for her hand in marriage, the pastor reminded Parsons of Sarah's "unpleasant temper." Parsons then asked, "She has grace, I trust?" Edwards replied with wit and wisdom, "I hope she has, but grace can live where you cannot."[118]

During the troubling 1740s Edwards received additional encouragement from his Scottish correspondents. Beginning in 1744, John M'Laurin of Glasgow, James Robe of Kilsyth, Thomas Gillespie, John Erskine, and others banded together to form a prayer union for the advancement of the gospel. Named the Concert for United Prayer, its design was to form a prayer network for intercession on behalf of the international extension of Christ's kingdom. These men earnestly sought worldwide revival through prayer. Their ardent desire was for God to "appear in his glory, and favour Zion, and manifest his compassion to the world of mankind, by an abundant effusion of his Holy Spirit on all the churches and the whole habitable earth, to revive true religion in all parts of Christendom and to deliver all nations from their great and manifold spiritual calamities and miseries."[119]

As word of the concert spread throughout Great Britain, John Wesley suggested that Edwards be invited to join. He heartily endorsed the plan. Writing to his friends in Scotland, he said, "Such an agreement and practice appears to me exceeding beautiful, and becoming Christians; and I doubt not but it is so in Christ's eyes."[120] Consequently, Edwards began to take "a great deal of pains to promote this concert here in America"[121] by preaching a series of sermons on Zechariah 8:20–22 and by forming private prayer groups in his church devoted to this purpose. He also revised his sermons for publication, and by January 1748 his book promoting the prayer concert was published as *An Humble Attempt to Promote Explicit Agreement and Visible Union of God's People in Extraordinary Prayer, for the Revival of Religion and the Advancement of Christ's Kingdom on Earth, Pursuant to Scripture-Promises and Prophecies Concerning the Last Time.* In this work, Edwards uttered his prophetic vision that the gospel of Christ would eventually spread "throughout all parts of Africa, Asia, America and Terra Australis"—a vision that has been largely realized.[122] Though Edwards was undoubtedly discouraged by the passing of the Great Awakening, he never lost faith in the power of the gospel and the promises of God.

Providentially, in May 1747, just as Edwards was polishing his missionary manuscript for the press, missionary David Brainerd rode into Northampton. The two had not seen each other since their first and only meeting at the Yale commencement of 1743, although Edwards had kept abreast of Brainerd's brief but blazing career. Around the time of the commencement, the Scotland's Society for Propagating Christian Knowledge hired Brainerd to be a missionary to American Indians. He was first sent to Kaunaumeek, twenty miles from Stockbridge, on the western borders of Massachusetts and New York. John Sargeant, a former student of Edwards, was working with the Indians at Stockbridge, and during the winter of 1743–44 he tutored Brainerd in Indian languages. After little visible success, Brainerd was sent to the Indians on the Delaware River in Pennsylvania, and by October he traveled west to the Susquehanna River. The following spring, Brainerd was fatigued, ill, and discouraged. While contemplating resignation in the summer of 1745, a revival took place among the Indians at Crossweeksung in New Jersey. For the next several months Brainerd labored furiously, riding three thousand miles on horseback in only nine months. However, he was so ill by late 1746 that he spent the winter months resting at the home of Jonathan Dickinson, then president of Princeton.

When Brainerd arrived in Northampton in the spring of 1747, his illness (probably tuberculosis) was far advanced. After a brief trip to Boston with Edwards's daughter Jerusha, Brainerd returned to Northampton for his final days. For the next few months he steadily and rapidly deteriorated, and on the morning of October 9, 1747, he died in Edwards's home. Before passing away, however, Brainerd gave his diaries and papers to Edwards to dispose of as he "thought would be most for God's glory and the interest of religion."[123] The result was Edwards's *An Account of the Life of the Late Reverend Mr. David Brainerd.* Published in 1749, this work became his most widely read and influential book.

Edwards's sadness at the death of Brainerd was compounded by the loss of two others close to him. The first was his daughter Jerusha. It seems that she served as Brainerd's nurse during his last days in the Northampton parsonage; sadly, she contracted tuberculosis from him. In February 1748 she fell ill. From her deathbed she told her family that "she had not seen one minute, for several years, wherein she desired to live one minute longer, for the sake of any other good in life, but doing good, living to God, and doing what might be for his glory." Five days later she died. Thus, only four months after Brainerd's death, Jerusha was laid to rest next to him.[124]

The second loss was his uncle John Stoddard (a son of Solomon Stoddard), who died in June of the same year. Colonel Stoddard had been the chief justice of the county and the leading citizen in Northampton. He reigned over the town like "the squire of an English village. No one else in the community had as much money as he or as much influence. He owned the first teapot in Northampton and the first gold watch."[125] In addition to being a county judge, he was a military commander against the French and Indians. Despite the conflicts in Northampton in the 1740s, Stoddard's support of Edwards's ministry shielded him from any direct opposition. In the words of Samuel Hopkins, Justice Stoddard "greatly strengthened" Edwards's hands. With his departure, however, Edwards lost his most influential backer in the town. Support for his ministry quickly faded. Moreover, now that Stoddard was gone, Edwards's critical cousin, Israel Williams, became the most prominent figure in the Connecticut Valley. As biographer Arthur C. McGiffert commented, Edwards was now "marked for punishment."[126]

The troubles brewing in Northampton now came to a boil in a "communion controversy." As mentioned earlier, Edwards had come to a position on church membership that differed from Solomon Stoddard's practice at Northampton. In essence, Edwards wanted applicants to make a public profession of saving faith or "godliness," not simply a profession of intellectual assent. Edwards drew up a "form of public profession":

> I hope I truly find in my heart a willingness to comply with all the commandments of God, which require me to give up myself wholly to him, and to serve him with my body and my spirit. And do accordingly now promise to walk in a way of obedience to all the commandments of God, as long as I live.[127]

In December 1748, an applicant for membership was told by Edwards that he must make a public "profession of godliness." He refused. As word of the incident spread, tension mounted in the town. Edwards was accused of "lording it over the flock" and of presuming to judge between "sheep and goats." At a church committee meeting in February 1749, Edwards suggested that he preach on the qualifications for membership. The committee objected but then agreed that Edwards should put his views in print. In the meantime, another applicant, Mary Hulbert, came to Edwards for admission. During the interview, she expressed her willingness to "publicly make a profession of religion." But by the time she returned for a second interview, she told Edwards that, based on what she had heard from others, she was afraid "there would be a tumult if she came into the church in that way." The issue was then referred to the committee of the church, which in April 1749 declined to approve Hulbert's making a public profession.

The dispute escalated. It was now clear that pastor and people were at odds on an important doctrinal point.

Therefore, Edwards informed the church committee that he would resign his post under two conditions. First, that the current members would wait to read his forthcoming book on the subject before voting, and second, that a "regular council" of ministers would approve his resignation (assuming the dispute could not be resolved). The committee agreed.

Edwards's book arrived in Northampton in August bearing the descriptive title *An Humble Inquiry into the Rules of the Word of God Concerning the Qualifications Requisite to a Complete Standing and Full Communion in the Visible Christian Church.* In the preface, he wrote: "I am conscious, not only is the interest of religion concerned in this affair, but my own reputation, future usefulness, and my very subsistence, all seem to depend on my freely opening and defending myself, as to my principles."[128] Never was Edwards more correct.

For a short time the controversy cooled, but in October 1749 two or three persons sought admission to the church. Strife again erupted. A resolution was passed in a town meeting threatening Edwards with dismissal if he persisted in his principles. By December a council of local ministers was convened to hear the dispute. Edwards appealed to the ministers to require his people to hear him preach on the subject since most of them had neglected to read his book. The request was rejected. Seeing the bias of the council due to the influence of the Williams clan, Edwards then asked that, should the conflict not be resolved, the next council be composed of some ministers from outside Hampshire County. Again the council refused.

Edwards keenly felt the intense malice toward him. Writing to his friend Joseph Bellamy, he said:

> Things are in great confusion: the tumult is vastly greater than when you were here, and is rising higher and higher continually. The people have got their resentments up to a great height. . . .
>
> I need God's counsel in every step I take and every word I speak; as all that I do and say is watched by the multitude around me with the utmost strictness and with eyes of the greatest uncharitableness and severity, and let me do or say what I will, my words and actions are represented in dark colours, and the state of things is come to that, that they seem to think it greatly concerns them to blacken me and represent me in odious colours to the world to justify their own conduct—they seem to be sensible that now their character can't stand unless it be on the ruin of mine.[129]

The hostility toward Edwards could hardly be the result of the doctrinal question in dispute. Rather, old resentment now had a pretense for spewing out its venom. Many of Edwards's opponents were related to the Williams family, and with Colonel Stoddard's death, Israel Williams became the chief citizen of Hampshire County. It was Williams, it should be remembered, who had bitterly attacked Edwards in 1734 for preaching against Arminianism. Four other ministers in the county were also part of the Williams family. Moreover, Joseph Hawley Jr., who took an active role against Edwards, had lost his father to suicide during the revival of 1734–35.

His attitude toward Edwards may have been colored by this as well as by the fact that Hawley had, in 1747, been at odds with Edwards on a case of church discipline involving his brother, Elisha. Deacon Ebenezer Pomeroy, another opponent of Edwards, had likewise sided with Hawley in that case. Thus, there was by 1748 a close-knit faction that opposed Edwards for personal reasons. Moreover, the great offense caused by the bad book case and the bad blood generated by the salary dispute had made Edwards "obnoxious" to his people.

After another council meeting in early February 1750, it was decided that Edwards would preach on the controversy during the Thursday lectures. Angry that Edwards was given a hearing, Noah Cook and Deacon Pomeroy sent a letter of protest to Chester Williams, a representative of the Hampshire association of ministers. The ministers convened briefly but took no action, so Edwards gave his lectures as scheduled. He began on February 15 and delivered five lectures that were thinly attended by his congregation, although many visitors were present. At the March 25 church meeting, a great majority indicated that their views on the subject had not changed; thus it was now necessary to choose a ministerial council to decide Edwards's fate. Desiring a fair hearing, Edwards demanded that he have a hand in choosing the members of the council. (He was clearly trying to avoid the predominance of the Williams family in Hampshire.) Not until May 3 was the question settled: the future council would include at least two ministers, chosen by Edwards, from outside Hampshire.

The decisive council convened in Northampton on June

19, 1750, and met for four days. They called a special church meeting where the people voted on Edwards's dismissal. Led by Joseph Hawley Jr., a heated majority voted for his removal. Though a minority of the council protested the people's hastiness, it was decided by a vote of ten to nine that Edwards's pastoral relation to Northampton church should be ended. Thus, after twenty-three years of diligent ministry, Edwards was publicly rejected by the people he had so faithfully served and so dearly loved.

Edwards received the verdict unshaken. As David Hall, a member of the council, jotted in his diary, "I never saw the least symptoms of displeasure in his countenance the whole week but he appeared like a man of God, whose happiness was out of the reach of his enemies."[130]

On July 1, 1750, only nine days after his dismissal, Edwards had to face his accusers and deliver a farewell sermon. Basing his message on 2 Corinthians 1:14—"As also ye have acknowledged us in part, that we are your rejoicing, even as ye also are ours in the day of the Lord Jesus"—he advised his former flock that both pastor and parishioners would one day stand before the judgment seat of Christ. At that day, God would examine the conduct of each in their respective treatment of one another. For his part, Edwards reminded the church that he had spent the best years of his life laboring on their behalf. "I have spent the prime of my life and strength in labours for your eternal welfare," he said. "You are my witnesses that what strength I have had, I have not neglected in idleness . . . but have given myself to the work of the ministry, labouring in it night and day, rising early, and applying myself to this great business to which Christ has appointed me." He also admonished them for their contentious spirit: "The contentions which have been among you, since I first became your pastor, have been one of the greatest burdens I have laboured under in the course of my ministry." This spirit, he warned, would "tend to drive away God's Spirit" from the church. "Let this late contention about the terms of Christian communion, as it has been the greatest, be the last."

Edwards then expressed his desire for their future welfare, asking that God might bless them with a faithful pastor, "one that is well acquainted with his mind and will, thoroughly warning sinners, wisely and skillfully searching professors and conducting you in the way to eternal blessedness." And finally, "Let us all remember, and never forget our future solemn meeting on the great day of the Lord; the day of infallible decision and of the everlasting and unalterable sentence. Amen."[131]

Many were moved by his tender but solemn address. Some were "much affected, and some are exceedingly grieved," noted Edwards. There may have even been "some relentings of heart" that they "voted me away."[132]

Such remorse notwithstanding, "away" Edwards went.

FRONTIER THEOLOGIAN

D ISMISSAL FROM THE NORTHAMPTON church left Edwards and his family without any means of support and with no prospects of employment. Writing in early July to his friend John Erskine, Edwards mused on his precarious situation: "I am now, as it were, thrown upon the wide ocean of the world, and know not what will become of me and my numerous and chargeable family. Nor have I any particular door in view that I depend upon to be opened for my future serviceableness." Despite the harsh treatment of his former flock and the unpromising outlook for the immediate future, Edwards steadfastly trusted in God: "We are in the hands of God, and I bless him, I am not anxious concerning his disposal."[133]

For the next several months Edwards was "unemployed." And it just so happened that the Northampton church was without a pastor—the supply committee being unable to locate a suitable replacement. So, strange as it sounds, Edwards was asked to occasionally fill the pulpit when another preacher could not be recruited. This he did at least twelve times over the next several months. On one occasion, two strangers who were prejudiced against Edwards visited Northampton and attended the Sabbath service. Since they had never before seen Edwards, they assumed the preacher that day was someone else. In the course of the sermon, one of the strangers whispered to his friend, "This is a *good* man." A little later in the sermon he leaned over and whispered again, "This is a *very good* man." Near the end, he was heard to say, "Whoever he may be, this is a *holy* man."[134]

Unfortunately, the majority at Northampton did not share the stranger's admiration for Edwards. Opponents objected to his supplying the pulpit, and the hostility toward him continued unabated. At a town meeting a vote was passed to deny him the use of the public grazing land, and it was finally agreed in November that it would be better to have no preacher rather than to have Edwards. He was plainly being railroaded out of town. Biographer Iain Murray noted, "So deep were their prejudices that their heat was maintained, nothing would quiet them till they could see the town clear of root and branch, name and remnant."[135]

A month later Edwards received a call to the Stockbridge Indian settlement, which had been founded as a missionary project of the London Society for Propagating the Gospel in New England. Colonel Stoddard, John

Sargeant, and Edwards himself were present at a meeting in Stoddard's home in 1734 when the decision was made to launch the settlement. It is not surprising, then, that Edwards entertained the invitation to labor there.

Accordingly, on a snowy day in January 1751, Edwards trekked to Stockbridge to inspect the situation firsthand. During the two-month visit, he found a small but thriving frontier village. About two hundred Housatonics lived there, with a school for their children run by Timothy Woodbridge. There was also a separate boarding school for the Mohawks, both young and old, run by John Kellogg. The church in Stockbridge was comprised of only a handful of white families and a slightly larger number of Indians.

The prospect of laboring, like Brainerd, as a missionary to the Indians was attractive to Edwards. For many years he had a genuine concern for the salvation and welfare of the native tribes. Stockbridge, it would seem, offered an ideal outlet for his vision of missionary expansion. Nonetheless, there were several obstacles to such a move. First, there was no parsonage in Stockbridge, and Edwards had no money to build one. Second, his potential salary would be far less than before. Third, Edwards knew no Indian language and would have to work through an interpreter. But the most significant objection to moving to Stockbridge was the presence of a branch of the Williams family. The leading landowner (four hundred acres) in Stockbridge was Ephraim Williams, an uncle of Solomon Williams, who differed with Edwards on the communion question and who had published a reply to Edwards's *Humble Inquiry.* Ephraim's daughter, Abigail, had been married to John Sargeant; and his son, Ephraim Jr., was the town's representative to the general court.

Back in Northampton by March, Edwards undoubtedly discussed the Stockbridge proposal with his wife, and they both surely sought God's guidance. During the next few months, Edwards's friends in Scotland sent him financial help, and probably much to Edwards's surprise, they asked the Edwardses to sit for portraits. Thankfully, Jonathan and Sarah cooperated immediately, and their portraits, now a great treasure to the church, were finished by the autumn of 1751. In the meantime, some of Edwards's friends in Northampton proposed a second church in town, with Edwards as pastor. Though he objected to the idea, his critics accused him of scheming to reestablish himself in Northampton in order to divide the existing church. This last attack was the worst. "Such is the state of things among us," wrote Edwards, "that a person cannot appear on my side without exposing himself to the resentments of his friends and neighbours, and being the object of much odium."[136]

Now convinced that it would be best for his family if they left town, Edwards went to Stockbridge in July and was officially installed as pastor on August 8, 1751. Sarah and the children soon followed in October. His family, by this time, was blessed with a third boy, Pierrepont. Also, his daughter Sarah had married Elihu Parsons in June 1750, and two months later Mary wed Timothy Dwight. Elihu and Sarah likewise moved to Stockbridge, while the Dwights stayed in Northampton. In protest of her father's dismissal, Mary never again took communion at the church.

Just as Edwards was getting settled in his new position, he again became embroiled in conflict. In early 1752, the Boston commissioners sent Gideon Hawley to Stockbridge to assume the oversight of the Mohawk school. Kellogg, the current director, had mismanaged the school for some time and was misappropriating funds sent from England. Not surprisingly, he contested his dismissal and resisted Hawley. Strife broke out, with Ephraim Williams supporting Kellogg, and Edwards supporting Hawley. By summer, Elisha Williams (Ephraim's nephew, once removed), a recently appointed member of the Boston commission, arrived in Stockbridge and demanded that Edwards answer directly to him. Edwards refused, insisting he was answerable to the entire commission, not just one of its members. Ill will increased to such a point that, by the winter of 1752, Joseph Dwight (Abigail Williams's new husband) petitioned the general court in an attempt to have Edwards removed. Simultaneously, Ephraim Williams Sr. tried to buy the land titles of Edwards's supporters in order to move them out of town. In February 1753, the Mohawk school, now under the oversight of Gideon Hawley, mysteriously burned to the ground, and all of Hawley's personal possessions were destroyed. Two months later he left town, with many Mohawks following. After nearly another year of discord, the Boston commission finally sided with Edwards. "He won a complete victory," wrote biographer Arthur C. McGiffert. "His persuasiveness and aggressiveness, reinforced by his reputation for integrity, saved the mission from further exploitation. . . . Ultimately he was himself given charge of the mission station, its funds, and its staff."[137]

Edwards also endured other difficulties on the frontier. The first problem was financial. Throughout this time, he and his family were financially strapped. The cost of moving to Stockbridge, the expense of marrying off two daughters, and his smaller missionary salary left Edwards in debt. In fact, Edwards was so desperate for a study notebook that he would sew together miscellaneous scraps of paper: "Printer's proofs, old proclamations of intended marriages from Northampton days, envelopes, letters, and much else, could all be utilized, even if there was only room on the margins or the bottoms of sheets."[138] His daughters, to help out, took up lace making, embroidery, and fan painting and sold their wares in Boston.

Another trial was family sickness. In late 1752, Edwards's wife, Sarah, was so ill that she nearly died. His daughter Betty "was brought nigh unto death," and Sarah Parsons likewise was very sick.[139] Edwards himself fell ill in the summer of 1754 with a case of malaria that lasted until January of the next year.

Of course, the perennial problem on the frontier was the threat of Indian attack. At the same time that Edwards was sick, some Indians from Canada swept into Stockbridge on a Sabbath and killed four men. The French and Indian War was just heating up, making Stockbridge a vulnerable frontier target. During these years it was not uncommon for soldiers to be garrisoned at Edwards's home. He often read his Bible to the rattle of bayonets.

In spite of all these obstacles, Edwards faithfully toiled as a missionary and theologian. He commonly conducted four services on each Sabbath: one for the Housatonics, one for the Mohawks, and two for his small white congregation. When preaching to the Indians, Edwards had to aim at simplicity, as can be seen from the sermon notes of one of his Indian sermons. Preaching on 2 Timothy 3:16, Edwards said:

> 'Tis worth the while to take a great deal of pains to learn to read and understand the Scriptures.
>
> I would have all of you think of this.
>
> When there is such a book that you may have, how can you be contented without being able to read it?
>
> How does it make you feel when you think there is a Book that is God's own Word? . . .
>
> You must not only hear the read, etc, but you must have it sunk down into your heart. Believe. Be affected. Love the Word of God.
>
> Must not only read and hear, but DO the things. Otherwise no good; but will be the worse for it.
>
> Consider how much it is worth the while to go often to your Bible to hear the great God Himself speak to you.[140]

On weekdays, Edwards taught classes on the Westminster Catechism and sacred history and instructed both white and Indian children in writing and spelling. There is certainly something touching, and ironic, in seeing America's most astute theologian tutoring children in the alphabet. Edwards, however, valuing humility as he did, was not above such tasks.

In some ways the move to Stockbridge, despite the hardships, was an unsought blessing. Compared to the bustle of activity and the burden of ministry in Northampton, Edwards's remote post was relatively quiet. There were fewer visitors to entertain and a smaller congregation to shepherd. God, in his good providence, provided Edwards with more time for deep theological reflection and study—and the result proved to be a rich blessing to the future church.

At Stockbridge, then, Edwards devoted himself to writing his greatest theological books. In November 1752, he published his last statement on the communion controversy, entitled *Misrepresentations Corrected.* Shortly thereafter, in August of the same year, he began writing *Careful and Strict Inquiry into the Modern Prevailing Notions of the Freedom of Will Which Is Supposed to Be Essential to Moral Agency.* Directed at the work of Thomas Chubb, Daniel Whitby, and Isaac Watts, it was Edwards's aim to refute the Arminian notion of human liberty and to show how God's sovereignty was compatible with human responsibility. This massive and intricate work has four sections. The first deals with the definition of such terms as "necessity," "contingency," "liberty," and many others. Part 2 is a critique of the Arminian view of liberty. Part 3 contains a discussion of whether freedom is essential to praise or blame. And in part 4 Edwards handles the arguments of his opponents.

Throughout the work, Edwards attempts to establish or prove two theses. First, he argues that God's certain foreknowledge of all that happens is inconsistent with the existence of contingency. Second, he argues that the volitions of the human soul of Jesus were necessarily holy, yet could still be called virtuous and praiseworthy. As scholar

John E. Smith noted: "The first of these theses was directed against the belief in self-determination or freedom of the will which Edwards associated with the Arminian thinkers. The second was meant to refute the belief that what is necessitated cannot be the object of praise or blame. The entire argument of the *Freedom of the Will* is directed to the establishment of these two claims."[141] Whether or not one agrees with Edwards's conclusions, Perry Miller is correct in suggesting that this work alone, due to its metaphysical majesty, was enough to establish Edwards as America's greatest philosopher-theologian.[142]

Next, in the winter and spring of 1754–55, Edwards composed two dissertations: *A Dissertation Concerning the End for Which God Ceated the World* and *A Dissertation Concerning the Nature of True Virtue.* Intended to be read together, the two dissertations are Edwards's answer to the Enlightenment's attempt to define virtue or morality apart from God. While some writers, such as Francis Hutcheson, acknowledged God in their ethical systems, it is clear that he did not see that God was foundational to morality. "There seems to be an inconsistence in some writers on morality, in this respect, that they do not wholly exclude a regard to the Deity out of their schemes of morality, but yet mention it so slightly, that they leave me room and reason to suspect they esteem it a less important and subordinate part of morality."[143] In effect, the trend of European moral philosophy at the time was to first limit and then exclude God from questions of morality.

Edwards, on the other hand, answered by saying that this approach was an inversion of the true order; namely, that we are required to love God first and supremely and mankind secondarily: "And it may be asserted in general, that nothing is of the nature of true virtue, in which God is not the *first* and *last;* or which, with regard to their exercises in general, have not their first foundation and source in apprehensions of God's supreme dignity and glory, and in answerable esteem and love of him, and have not respect to God as the supreme end."[144]

Edwards's last major theological work, *The Great Christian Doctrine of Original Sin Defended,* was begun in 1756 and published in early 1758. The occasion of the book was twofold. First, Edwards was responding to John Taylor's book *The Scripture-Doctrine of Original Sin Proposed to Free and Candid Examination.* But perhaps more significantly, Edwards saw the Enlightenment bias that ignored man's innate depravity and exalted his inherent goodness. But if man is not a sinner, then he needs no atonement, no gospel, and no Christ. Using both reason and revelation, Edwards established an arsenal of arguments showing that all men—civilized Europeans and "savage" Indians alike—are indeed sinners in need of Christ's atonement.

While working on *Original Sin,* Edwards received a letter from Aaron Burr, president of the College of New Jersey (now Princeton), informing him of a revival at the school. Burr was Edwards's son-in-law, having married the pastor's daughter Esther in September 1752. Over the years, Burr and Edwards had stayed in contact, and on several occasions Edwards had visited the college. In September 1755, for instance, Edwards was the guest speaker at the college commencement. When word arrived in February 1757 of the awakening among the students, Edwards was overjoyed and passed on the good news to his friends in Scotland.

Unfortunately, Edwards's joy was short-lived. Six months later he learned that Governor Belcher, a strong supporter of the school, had passed away. Then, to the shock of everyone connected with the institution, Burr died a month later at the age of forty-one. Esther, now a widow, found her solace in God. Writing home to Stockbridge, she commented on God's grace to her during this tragic time: "God has seemed sensibly near in such a supporting and comfortable manner that I think I have never experienced the like."[145]

Only four days after Burr's death, Princeton's board of trustees chose Edwards as his successor. When news arrived in Stockbridge, Edwards wrote a long letter (dated October 19, 1757) of objections to the invitation. First, Edwards thought the move to Princeton would be a discomfort to his family, especially since they had only recently settled in Stockbridge. Another move, he thought, might produce further financial strain. More important, Edwards felt that he was unfit for the position of president:

> The chief difficulties in my mind, in the way of accepting this important and arduous office, are these two: First, my own defects unfitting me for such an undertaking, many of which are generally known; beside others of which my own heart is conscious—I have a constitution, in many respects, peculiarly unhappy, attended with . . . a low tide of spirits; often occasioning a kind of childish weakness and contemptibleness of speech, presence, and

demeanour, with a disagreeable dullness and stiffness, much unfitting me for conversation, but more especially for the government of a college. This makes me shrink at the thoughts of taking upon me, in the decline of life, such a new and great business, attended with such a multiplicity of cares, and requiring such a degree of activity, alertness, and spirit of government; especially as succeeding one so remarkably well qualified in these respects, giving occasion to every one to remark the wide difference. I am also deficient in some parts of learning, particularly in algebra, and the higher parts of mathematics, and the Greek classics; my Greek learning having been chiefly in the New Testament.[146]

Edwards then informed the trustees that he was thoroughly enjoying his reclusive studies and had no desire to be yanked from his books: "My engaging in this business will not well consist with those views, and that course of employ in my study, which have long engaged and swallowed up my mind, and been the chief entertainment and delight of my life." In addition to continued projects relating to the debate between Arminians and Calvinists, Edwards was also planning a new body of divinity.

I have had on my mind and heart (which I long ago began, not with any view to publication) a great work, which I call a *History of the Work of Redemption,* a body of divinity in an entire new method, being thrown into the form of a history; considering the affair of Christian theology, as the whole of it, each part, stands in reference to the great work of redemption by Jesus Christ; which I suppose to be, of all others, the grand design of God, and the *summum* and *ultimum* of all the divine operations and decrees; particularly considering all parts of the grand scheme, in their historical order.[147]

Edwards concluded his objections by mentioning another work, *Harmony of the Old and New Testament,* writing, "So far as I myself am able to judge of what talents I have for benefiting my fellow creatures by word, I think I can write better than I can speak. My heart is so much in these studies that I cannot find it in my heart to be willing to put myself into an incapacity to pursue them any more in the future part of my life."[148]

Nevertheless, Edwards did mention that if he should ever come to accept the position, he would only do the work of a professor of divinity. And if the trustees still wanted to pursue the matter with him, he would seek the advice of some trusted friends.

In light of Edwards's outstanding gifts as a theologian and philosopher, it is not surprising that Princeton persisted in its invitation. Accordingly, Edwards called a council of friends to advise him on the matter. Samuel Hopkins, John Brainerd, and Joseph Bellamy were asked to come to Stockbridge in late December 1757. Due to weather, perhaps, the council did not meet until January 4, 1758. After Edwards presented his view of the matter, Timothy Woodbridge added his arguments for keeping Edwards at Stockbridge. In spite of their persuasive pleading, the council informed Edwards that it was his duty to accept the call to Princeton. He was stunned and broke into tears. Nevertheless, believing that he was bound to heed their advice, he submitted to their counsel and prepared to depart for Princeton.

In late January, Edwards gave his last Stockbridge sermon on the words, "We have no continuing city, therefore let us seek one to come." Little did he realize, when he made that wintry trip to Princeton, just how prophetic those words would prove to be.

An Unhappy Providence

*E*DWARDS WAS OFFICIALLY INSTALLED as president of Princeton College on February 16, 1758. Despite his previous apprehensions, he settled into his new routine with alacrity. His duties included preaching on the Sabbath in the college hall and quizzing the senior class on questions of theology. For instance, he might ask his students the following questions:

- How do you prove the natural perfection of God, viz., his intelligence, infinite power, foreknowledge, and immutability?
- How do you prove the divinity of Christ?
- What is the true idea of God's decrees?
- Are the law and gospel inconsistent with each other?
- What is the covenant of redemption?
- What is regeneration?

- What is pardon and justification? What is their foundation, and what is the influence of faith therein?[149]

By all accounts, the students were thrilled with his instruction.

A week after his installation, Edwards was advised to
be inoculated for smallpox. Since the disease was then
prevalent and Edwards had not before contracted it, he
complied. For a brief time all seemed well. But several
weeks later he came down with the disease, and his
health rapidly declined. He was unable to take fluids and
a fever ravished his body. As he wrestled with death, Edwards called for his daughter Lucy, to whom he said:

> It seems to me to be the will of God, that I must shortly
> leave you; therefore give my kindest love to my dear
> wife, and tell her, that the uncommon union, which has
> so long subsisted between us, has been of such a nature,
> as I trust is spiritual, and therefore will continue for ever.
> And I hope she will be supported under so great a trial
> and submit cheerfully to the will of God. And as to my
> children, you are now like to be left fatherless, which I
> hope will be an inducement to you all, to seek a Father
> who will never fail you.[150]

Sensing that his departure was near, Edwards looked
about the room at his gathered friends and family members and said: "Now where is Jesus of Nazareth, my true
and never-failing friend?" He then fell into a semi-
conscious state. Observing this, and thinking he had died,
those at his bedside began to grieve. Then, unexpectedly,

Edwards exclaimed: "Trust in God, and you need not fear!" Thus, on March 22, 1758, Edwards gave his final witness to the God he had faithfully served for many years.

On March 22, 1758, Edwards's doctor, William Shippen, wrote to Sarah of her husband's passing.

Most Dear and Very Worthy Madam,

I am heartily sorry for the occasion of writing to you, by this express, but I know you have been informed, by a line from your excellent, lovely, and pious husband, that I was brought here to inoculate him, and your dear daughter Esther, and her children, for the smallpox, which was then spreading fast in Princeton; and that, after the most deliberate and serious consultation, with his nearest and most religious friends, he was accordingly inoculated with them the 23d of last month; and although he had the smallpox favorably, yet, having a number of them in the roof of his mouth and throat, he could not possibly swallow a sufficient quantity of drink, to keep off a secondary fever, which has proved too strong for his feeble frame; and this afternoon, between two and three o'clock, it pleased God to let him sleep in that dear Lord Jesus, whose kingdom and interest he has been faithfully and painfully serving all his life. And never did any mortal man more fully and clearly evidence the sincerity of all his professions, by one continued, universal, calm, cheerful resignation, and patient submission to the Divine will, through every stage of his disease, than he; not so much as one discontented expression nor the least appearance of murmuring, through the whole. And never did any

person expire with more perfect freedom from pain;—
not so much as one distorted hair—but in the most
proper sense of the words, he fell asleep. Death had certainly lost its sting, as to him.

I conclude, with my hearty prayer, dear Madam, that
you may be enabled to look to that God, whose love and
goodness you have experienced a thousand times, for direction and help, under this most afflictive dispensation of
his providence, and under every other difficulty, you may
meet with here, in order to your being more perfectly fitted for the joys of heaven hereafter.[151]

Sarah Edwards's April 3 response, written to Esther in
Princeton, shows both the depth of her faith in God and
her insight that, though her husband was now dead, his
work would continue.

My Very Dear Child,
What shall I say? A holy and good God has covered us
with a dark cloud. O that we may kiss the rod, and lay
our hands on our mouths! The Lord has done it. He has
made me adore his goodness, that we had him so long.
But my God lives; and he has my heart. O what a legacy
my husband, and your father, has left us! We are all given
to God; and there I am, and love to be.[152]

A day after his death, Edwards was given a simple bur-
ial at Princeton. Six months later Sarah joined her husband in the grave.

By colonial standards Edwards lived a full and rich life.
He had been an instructor, a pastor, a revivalist, a mission-

ary, a theologian-philosopher, and a college president. He was a powerful instrument in the most powerful revival of his day and a leading polemicist in the leading controversies of his time. He was a spiritual giant in a day when spirituality was highly prized: a burning and shining star amid a constellation of lesser lights. He had an "uncommon union" with his beloved wife and delighted in the familial fellowship of his many children. His quiver was full; his life had been blessed.

When Edwards died, he had no regrets, only expectation. His unfinished manuscripts were mere shadows compared to the light that lay before him. Loving Jesus as he did—his "true and never-failing friend"—Edwards welcomed death as the gateway to everlasting joy. Being his whole life so heavenly minded, how could he now mind going to heaven?

Edwards's unexpected death at the hand of his own physician, as well as his short-lived tenure as president of Princeton, may seem a tragic ending to such a noble life. Yet we are in God's hands, and how he disposes of his servants is beyond our finite grasp. Why Brainerd, for instance, should die of tuberculosis at the height of his missionary activity, or Edwards should succumb to a vaccine when on the brink of national, if not international, recognition as a college president and theologian, are questions no one can answer. The secret things belong to the Lord. It is enough for us to answer with Sarah, "The Lord has done it."

PART 2

THE CHARACTER OF JONATHAN EDWARDS

Mr. Edwards is a solid, excellent Christian. . . . I think I have not seen his fellow in all New England.

—GEORGE WHITEFIELD

The greatest, wisest, humblest and holiest of uninspired men.

—JOHN RYLAND

Never was there a happier combination of great power with great piety.

—THOMAS CHALMERS

There are two ways of recommending true religion and virtue in the world, which God hath made use of: the one is by doctrine and precept; the other by instance and example.

—JONATHAN EDWARDS

BOOKS

I make it my rule to lay hold of light and embrace it, wherever I see it, though held forth by a child or an enemy.—Jonathan Edwards

*J*ONATHAN EDWARDS WAS FIRST and foremost a thinker. True, he acted when action was needed, but very often he acted through the medium of his pen. In other words, he was leader by virtue of his intellectual perception and power.

Edwards's life as a pastor was, apart from a few years of remarkable revival, a relatively staid and regular course. He was a man of routine, both in and out of the pulpit. His most memorable and lasting achievements were those he accomplished with his mind. Thus, Edwards was a man who was shaped by the written word. He was a "voracious, intense, wide-ranging, and engaging reader"[1] who, according to an early biographer, was "devoted to books from his infancy."[2]

As we have already noted, Edwards was well acquainted with the standard Puritan divines. I use the word *standard* here not in a condescending way but to say that the authors whom Edwards read were widely recognized as sound, orthodox, Calvinist theologians. Here is a sampling:

- Henry Ainsworth, *Annotations Upon the First Book of Moses Called Genesis*
- William Ames, *Medulla Theologica* and other works
- Richard Baxter, *The Saints Everlasting Rest*
- Thomas Boston, *Human Nature in Its Fourfold State; The Mystery of Christ; The Sovereignty and Wisdom of God Displayed in the Affliction of Men*
- Anthony Burgess, *The Doctrine of Original Sin, Asserted and Vindicated,* etc.
- Stephen Charnock, *Works*
- Jonathan Dickinson, *The True Scripture Doctrine Concerning Some Important Points of the Christian Faith,* etc.
- John Flavel, *Husbandry Spiritualized; Pneumatologia;* others
- Thomas Fuller, *Works*
- Thomas Goodwin, *Works*
- Matthew Henry, *Exposition of the Old and New Testament; Communicant's Companion*
- John Howe, *Works*
- Thomas Manton, *Psalm 119; Commentary on James; Sermons*
- Cotton Mather, *Manuductio ad Ministerium*
- John Owen, *The Doctrine of Justification by Faith*

Through the Imputation of the Righteousness of Christ; Exercitations on the Epistle to the Hebrews; Discourse on the Holy Spirit; others

- William Perkins, *Works*
- Matthew Poole, *Synopsis Criticorum Aliorumque Sacrae Scripturae Interpretum; Annotations upon the Holy Bible*
- John Preston, *A Heavenly Treatise of the Divine Love of Christ;* others
- Thomas Ridgley, *Body of Divinity; The Doctrine of Original Sin*
- Thomas Shepard, *The Parable of the Ten Virgins Opened and Applied; The Sound Believer;* others
- Richard Sibbes, *The Bruised Reed and Smoking Flax*
- Solomon Stoddard, *A Treatise Concerning Conversion;* others
- Robert Traill, *A Vindication of the Protestant Doctrine Concerning Justification,* etc.

In addition to the Puritans, Edwards read older theologians such as Petrus van Mastricht (*Theoretico-Practica Theologia*), Francis Turretin (*Institutes of Elenctic Theology*), and Jerome Zanchius while at the same time reading contemporaries like Isaac Watts, Phillip Doddridge, and many others. Edwards's curious and probing mind led him to read in many different fields, not just theology alone. He read skeptics like David Hume, the great Protestant poet John Milton, and renowned philosophers such as John Locke and Isaac Newton.

As diffuse as his reading was, Edwards realized the need to make all subservient to the Bible. He determined "to read the Bible daily, and to read it in connexion with other religious books, diligently and attentively."[3] In his *Diary* he wrote in 1723: "I find it would be very much to my advantage, to be thoroughly acquainted with the Scriptures. When I am reading doctrinal books, or books of controversy, I can proceed with abundantly more confidence; can see on what footing and foundation I stand."[4] Edwards's devotion to theology was essential to his calling as a pastor-scholar. Like every great leader, he understood that he needed to master the body of knowledge required by his vocation. Edwards did just that, and as a result he not only was shaped by the past but he shaped the future of his discipline.

STUDY

I am fitted for no other business but study.—
Jonathan Edwards

EDWARDS'S READING WAS NOT simply a leisurely pastime. He was not a "man of letters" as were some English gentlemen. While he may have at times done some "light reading," for the most part, Edwards was working when he was reading. In other words, he would not only read, he would study. The difference between the two is incalculable. Reading may be done passively, with little or no effort; study requires hard work. Reading may be done impulsively; study demands discipline. Reading may lead to scanty knowledge; study yields wisdom.

It was Edwards's opinion that study—at a minimum, study of the Scriptures—was an indispensable part of being a Christian. In his sermon "The Importance and Advantage of a Thorough Knowledge of Divine Truth" (November 1739), Edwards expounds the text in Hebrews

5:12—"For when for the time ye ought to be teachers, ye have need that one teach you again which be the first principles of the oracles of God; and are become such as have need of milk, and not of strong meat." He says in the introduction: "We may observe wherein the fault of this defect appears, viz., in that they [the Hebrews] had not made proficiency according to their time. For the time, they ought to have been teachers. As they were Christians, their business was to learn and gain Christian knowledge. They were scholars in the school of Christ."[5]

The doctrine or thesis of the sermon was thus: "Every Christian should make a business of endeavoring to grow in knowledge of divinity." By "divinity" Edwards meant "that science or doctrine which comprehends all those truths and rules which concern the great business of religion." Or, as he says later: "Divinity comprehends all that is taught in the Scriptures, and so all that we need know, or is to be known, concerning God and Jesus Christ, concerning our duty to God, and our happiness in God."[6] Every Christian does not just minister but must also study divinity. "The things of divinity not only concern ministers, but are of infinite importance to all Christians." Indeed, "Consider yourselves as scholars or disciples, put into the school of Christ; and therefore be diligent to make proficiency in Christian knowledge. Content not yourselves with this, that you have been taught your catechism in your childhood, and that you know as much of the principles of religion as is necessary to salvation. So you will be guilty of what the apostle warns against, viz., going no further than laying the foundation of repentance from dead works, etc."

To this end, Edwards exhorted his members to first "be assiduous in reading the holy Scriptures." The key word, of course, is *assiduous.* Read the Word frequently and intensely. Second, "Content not yourselves with only a cursory reading, without regarding the sense. This is an ill way of reading, to which, however, many accustom themselves all their days." Here, Edwards is hitting on the important distinction between reading and studying. To understand "the sense" demands sustained thinking. He continues: "When you read, observe what you read. Observe how things come in. Take notice of the drift of the discourse, and compare one Scripture with another. . . . We are expressly directed by Christ to *search* the Scriptures, which evidently intends something more than a mere cursory reading."

Just as Bible study means more than reading, it often requires the use of additional books as aids to understanding a text or doctrine. So Edwards implores his congregants to purchase and diligently read good doctrinal books:

> Procure, and diligently use other books which may help you to grow in this knowledge. There are many excellent books extant, which might greatly forward you in this knowledge, and afford you a very profitable and pleasant entertainment in your leisure hours. There is doubtless a great defect in many [persons], that through a loathness to be at a little expense, they furnish themselves with no more helps of this nature. They have a few books indeed, which now and then on Sabbath days they read; but they have had them so long, and read them so often, that they

are weary of them, and it is now become a dull story, a mere task to read them.

Happily, Edwards practiced what he preached. He not only read, he studied. According to his first biographer, he spent more than twelve hours a day in his study. While perhaps a laborious task at first, Edwards learned to love study. When later in 1757 he was asked to take the presidency of Princeton, he declined the offer for two reasons. The first was his declining health. The second, however, was his love of study. He was not at all eager to take upon himself either teaching or administrative duties that would pull him away from his reading and writing. As he wrote to the trustees of the college in October 1757:

> The other thing [objection] is this; that my engaging in this business will not well consist with those views, and that course of employ in my study, which have long engaged and swallowed up my mind, and been the chief entertainment and delight of my life.
>
> My method of study, from my first beginning the work of the ministry, has been very much by writing, applying myself, in this way, to improve every important hint; pursuing the clue to my utmost, when any thing in reading, meditation, or conversation, has been suggested to my mind, that seemed to promise light, in any weighty point—thus penning what appeared to me my best thoughts, on innumerable subjects, for my own benefit. The longer I prosecuted my studies in this method, the more habitual it became, and the more pleasant and profitable I found it.[7]

Edwards's study, of course, yielded some of the greatest works in American philosophy and theology. But his habit also serves as a model to all of us, especially those who aspire to leadership. To lead you must read. And by read I mean study and think. There is no shortcut to knowledge and wisdom. And without them, one cannot be a leader.

DISCIPLINE

Resolved, to study the Scriptures so steadily,
constantly and frequently, as that I may find, and
plainly perceive myself to grow in knowledge of
the same.—Jonathan Edwards

EDWARDS'S HABIT OF STUDY was possible only because he was a man of great discipline. He trained himself to think and to regulate other areas of his life with his goal of study in view. This meant being disciplined in all aspects of his life.

Sereno Dwight, Edwards's descendant and author of the *Memoir* prefaced to the two-volume edition of Edwards's *Works,* gives us an intimate picture of the discipline that Edwards imposed upon himself to be a faithful pastor and scholar:

Immediately after his settlement [at Northampton], Mr. Edwards commenced the practice of preparing two discourses weekly; one of which was preached as a lecture, on an evening in the week. This he continued for several years. Though he regarded preaching the gospel as the great duty of a minister, and would on no account offer to God, or deliver to his people, that which was not the fruit of toil and labour; yet he resolved, from the commencement of his ministry, not to devote the time of each week exclusively to the preparation of his sermons, but to spend a large portion of it in the study of the Bible, and in the investigation of the more difficult and important subjects of theology. . . . With an infirm constitution, and health ordinarily feeble, it was obviously impossible, however, to carry this resolution into practice, without the most strict attention to diet, exercise, and method; but in all these points, his habits had long been formed, and persevered in, with a direct reference to the best improvement of time, and the greatest efficiency of his intellectual powers. In eating and drinking, he was unusually abstemious, and constantly watchful. He carefully observed the effects of the different sorts of food, and selected those which best suited his constitution, and rendered him most fit for mental labour. Having also ascertained the quantity of food, which, while it sustained his bodily strength, left his mind most sprightly and active, he most scrupulously and exactly confined himself to the prescribed limits; regarding it as a shame and a sin, to waste his time, and his mental strength, by animal indulgence. In this respect, he lived by rule, and constantly practiced great self-denial; as he did, also, with regard to the time passed in sleep. He accustomed himself to rise at four, or between four and five, in the morning, and, in winter, spent several of those hours in study which are commonly wasted in slumber.[8]

As a pastor, Edwards was obliged to spend time with his people, yet he did not frequently visit his congregation house to house as was the custom of many pastors in his day. Edwards knew that he was deficient in "entertaining" people, in making small talk. Instead, he realized that his gifts lent themselves to study and reflection. He did, however, encourage his people to visit him in his study, especially when they were under "religious impressions."

According to biographer Dwight:

> Owing to his constant watchfulness and self-denial in food and sleep, and his regular attention to bodily exercise, notwithstanding the feebleness of his constitution, few students are capable of more close or more long-continued application than he was. He commonly spent thirteen hours every day in his study; and these hours were passed, not in perusing or treasuring up the thoughts of others, but in employments far more exhausting—in the investigation of difficult subjects, in the origination and arrangement of thoughts, in the invention of arguments, and in the discovery of truths and principles. Nor was his exact method, in the distribution of his time, of less essential service. In consequence of his uniform regularity and self-denial, and the force of habit, the powers of his mind were always at his command, and would do their prescribed task in the time appointed.[9]

As a result of Edwards's discipline, he was able to not only prepare his weekly sermons and lectures, but he filled numerous notebooks (his *Miscellanies, Notes on Scripture,* etc.) with valuable insights to use later in his sermons and books. This was how he was able in his later years at Stockbridge to write his famous works on original sin and free will. He had for years disciplined himself to study and hoarded his meditations for future use. As with every great leader, discipline was at the foundation of his success.

CONSECRATION

*Such little things as Christians commonly do, will
not evince much increase of grace. We must do
great things for God.—Jonathan Edwards*

*E*VERY GREAT LEADER HAS a master passion. For
Edwards, that passion was to bring God glory
by devoting himself unreservedly to God. He intended to
live, not as the masses of Christians do—halfhearted and
lukewarm—but to live a life of total dedication to the revealed will of God. To this end, Edwards consecrated all
that he was and all that he had to the service of God.

Nowhere is this consecration better seen than in the
journal entry of January 12, 1723, which he wrote at the
beginning of his ministerial career. What it reveals is a
man who is earnest to master himself and serve God.
Nothing halfhearted here! It is all or nothing for God.

I have this day, solemnly renewed my baptismal covenant
and self-dedication, which I renewed when I was taken
into the communion of the church. I have been before

God, and have given myself, all that I am and have, to
God; so that I am not, in any respect, my own. I can challenge no right in this understanding, this will, these affections, which are in me. Neither have I any right to this
body, or any of its members—no right to this tongue,
these hands, these feet; no right to these senses, these
eyes, these ears, this smell, or this taste. I have given myself clear away, and have not retained any thing as my
own. I gave myself to God in my baptism, and I have
been this morning to him, and told him, that I gave myself *wholly* to him. I have given every power to him; so
that, for the future, I'll challenge no right in myself, in no
respect whatever. I have expressly promised him, and I
do now promise Almighty God, that by his grace I will
not. I have this morning told him that I did take him for
my whole portion and felicity, looking on nothing else as
any part of my happiness, nor acting as if it were; and his
law, for the constant rule of my obedience; and would
fight with all my might against the world, the flesh, and
the devil, to the end of my life; and that I did believe in
Jesus Christ, and did receive him as a Prince and Saviour;
and that I would adhere to the faith and obedience of the
gospel, however hazardous and difficult the confession
and practice of it may be; and that I did receive the
blessed Spirit and my Teacher, Sanctifier, and only Com-
forter, and cherish all his motions to enlighten, purify,
confirm, comfort, and assist me. This, I have done; and I
pray God, for the sake of Christ, to look upon it as a self-
dedication, and to receive me now as entirely his own,
and to deal with me, in all respects, as such, whether he
afflicts me or prospers me, or whatever he pleases to do

with me, who am his. How, henceforth, I am not to act, in any respect, as my own.[10]

Here is the true secret of Edwards's greatness: apart from the power of God's Spirit he was nothing. Edwards learned this from experience. Nevertheless, for his part, he was willing to surrender all to God. And the result was that God received the offering and used Edwards's life to bring multitudes to a saving knowledge of Christ and also to edify the body of Christ for ages to come.

DETERMINATION

*Being sensible that I am unable to do anything
without God's help, I do humbly entreat him by
his grace to enable me to keep these Resolutions,
so far as they are agreeable to his will, for Christ's
sake.—Jonathan Edwards*

DWARDS'S DESIRE TO BE fully consecrated to
God led him to draft a series of resolutions.
Consecration and growth in holiness were not one-time
acts; they required a daily determination to live according
to the principles revealed in Scripture. Indeed, reflecting
back on his solemn act of dedication to God in January
1723, Edwards said: "But I have reason to be infinitely
humbled, when I consider how much I have failed of an-
swering my obligation."[11]

Nevertheless, he was determined, in spite of repeated
failures, to make his consecration a daily reality. There is
no better way to appreciate his determination to live for
God than to let some of his resolutions speak for him.

1. Resolved, that I will do whatsoever I think to be
   most to God's glory, and my own good, profit and

pleasure in the whole of my duration [life], without any consideration of the time, whether now, or never so many myriads of ages hence.

4. Resolved, never to do any manner of thing, whether in soul or body, less or more, but what tends to the glory of God; not be, nor suffer it, if I can avoid it.

5. Never to lose one moment of time, but to improve it in the most profitable way I possibly can.

6. To live with all my might, while I do live.

7. Resolved, never to do anything, which I should be afraid to do, if it were the last hour of my life.

10. Resolved, when I feel pain, to think of the pains of martyrdom, and of hell.

13. Resolved, to be endeavoring to find out fit objects of charity and liberality.

14. Resolved, never to any thing out of revenge.

15. Resolved, never to suffer the least motions of anger towards irrational beings.

16. Resolved, never to speak evil of any one, so that I shall tend to his dishonour, more of less, upon no account except for some real good.

17. Resolved, that I will live so, as I shall wish I had done when I come to die.

18. Resolved, to live so, at all times, as I think is best in my devout frames, and when I have clearest motions of things of the gospel, and another world.

19. Resolved, never to do any thing, which I should be afraid to do, if I expected it would not be above an hour before I should hear the last trump.

20. Resolved, to maintain the strictest temperance in eating and drinking.

25. Resolved, to examine carefully, and constantly, what that one thing in me is, which causes me in the least to doubt of the love of God; and to direct all my forces against it.
30. Resolved, to strive to my utmost every week to be brought higher in religion, and to a higher exercise of grace, than I was the week before.
31. Resolved, never to say anything at all against anybody, but when it is perfectly agreeable to the highest degree of Christian honor, and of love to mankind, agreeable to the lowest humility, and a sense of my own faults and failings, and agreeable to the golden rule.
37. Resolved, to inquire every night, as I am going to bed, wherein I have been negligent,—what sin I have committed,—and wherein I have denied myself;—also, at the end of every week, month, and year.
41. Resolved, to ask myself, at the end of every day, week, month, and year, wherein I could possibly, in any respect, have done better.
42. Resolved, frequently to renew the dedication of myself to God, which was made at my baptism, which I solemnly renewed when I was received into the communion of the church, and which I have solemnly remade this 12th day of January, 1723.
43. Resolved, never, henceforward, till I die, to act as if I were any way my own, but entirely and altogether God's.
44. Resolved, that no other end but religion shall have any influence at all on any of my actions; and that

no action shall be, in the least circumstance, any otherwise than the religious end will carry it.

53. Resolved, to improve every opportunity, when I am in the best and happiest frame of mind, to cast and venture my soul on the Lord Jesus Christ, to trust and confide in him, and consecrate myself wholly to him; that from this I may have assurance of my safety, knowing that I confide in my Redeemer.[12]

Many similar resolutions could be cited, seeing that Edwards penned seventy of them. Yet they clearly reveal a heart that is determined to dedicate all and sacrifice all for God. It was this kind of determination that made Edwards a fit tool in the hand of God for great spiritual revival—that made him, in effect, a great spiritual leader.

SPIRITUALITY

The mind having a sensibleness of the excellency of divine objects, dwells upon them with delight; and the powers of the soul are more awakened and enlivened to employ themselves in the contemplation of them, and exert themselves more fully and much more to the purpose.—Jonathan Edwards

THAT EDWARDS WAS A great intellect is disputed by none. Indeed, he is considered by many to be the greatest intellect ever born on American soil. That is quite a statement when we consider that America, in the colonial period alone, produced such intellectuals as Cotton Mather, Benjamin Franklin, Thomas Jefferson, John Marshall, and John Adams, just to mention a few.

Through the centuries, the church of Christ has produced many men of mighty intellect. We can think, for instance, of Augustine, Aquinas, Luther, and Calvin. But what makes Edwards such a daunting figure and challenging example is not merely his intellect but also his profound spirituality. His mind was on fire with the Spirit of God. As the modern expositor Martyn Lloyd-Jones noted:

> An American of the name of [Richard] Hofstadter published a book in the 1960's entitled *Anti-Intellectualism in American Life*. Some English Evangelicals seem to have discovered this recently, and reversing their previous practice, are now telling us to put great emphasis upon the intellect. The answer to that, once more, is to read Jonathan Edwards. It is not anti-intellectualism. You cannot use the term anti-intellectualism when you are talking about Jonathan Edwards! It is quite the reverse; in him you have an intellect fired by, and filled with, the Holy Spirit.[13]

Elsewhere, Lloyd-Jones referred to Edwards's "mighty intellect, accompanied by a brilliant imagination" and "amazing originality." Yet "with all those scintillating gifts there is his humility and modesty, and added to that his exceptional spirituality."[14] Accordingly, Lloyd-Jones believed that the secret of Edwards was this: "The spiritual always controlled the intellectual in him."[15] Well-known Princeton theologian Benjamin B. Warfield concurred. He said that Edwards "stands out as the one figure of real greatness in the intellectual life of colonial America."[16] Yet he also noted that "the peculiarity of Edwards's theological work is due to the union in it of the richest religious sentiment with the highest intellectual powers."[17]

Edwards's exceptional spirituality can be seen in the intimate communion that he held with God. As he revealed in his *Personal Narrative:*

I have sometimes had a sense of the excellent fullness of
Christ, and his meetness and suitableness as a Saviour;
whereby he has appeared to me, far above all, the chief of
ten thousands. His blood and atonement have appeared
sweet, and his righteousness sweet; which was always
accompanied with ardency of spirit; and inward strugglings and breathings, and groanings that cannot be uttered, to be emptied of myself, and swallowed up in
Christ.[18]

He continued the same narrative:

Once, as I rode out into the woods for my health, in 1737,
having alighted from my horse in a retired place, as my
manner commonly has been, to walk for divine contemplation and prayer, I had a view, that for me was extraordinary, of the glory of the Son of God, as Mediator between
God and man, and his wonderful, great, full, pure and
sweet grace and love, and meek and gentle condescen-
sion. This grace that appeared so calm and sweet, appeared also great above the heavens. The person of Christ
appeared ineffably excellent, with an excellency great
enough to swallow up all thought and conception—
which continued, as near as I can judge, about an hour;
which kept me the greater part of the time in a flood of
tears, and weeping aloud. I felt an ardency of soul to be,
what I know not otherwise how to express, emptied and
annihilated; to lie in the dust, and to be full of Christ
alone; to love him with a holy and pure love; to trust in
him; to live upon him; to serve and follow him; and to be
perfectly sanctified and made pure, with a divine and

heavenly purity. I have several other times had views very much of the same nature, and which have had the same effects.[19]

These are hardly the sentiments, or experiences, of an abstract intellectual. In fact, Edwards believed and argued that true knowledge, that is, knowledge of spiritual things in the biblical sense, was more than a mere theoretical grasp of the mind. He observed: "The things of religion take place in men's hearts, no further than they are affected with them. The informing of the understanding is all vain, any farther that it affects the heart, or, which is the same thing, has influence on the affections."[20]

In his famous sermon titled "A Divine and Supernatural Light, Immediately Imparted to the Soul by the Spirit of God," Edwards explained the difference between an intellectual grasp of truth and a spiritual perception of it. Spiritual and divine light is

a true sense of the divine and superlative glory in these things; an excellency that is of vastly higher kind, and more sublime nature, than in other things; a glory greatly distinguishing them from all that is earthly and temporal. He that is spiritually enlightened truly apprehends and sees it, or has a sense of it. He does not merely rationally believe that God is glorious, but he has a sense of the gloriousness of God in his heart. There is not only a rational belief that God is holy, and that holiness is a good thing, but there is a sense of the loveliness of God's holiness. There is not only a speculatively judging that God is gracious, but a sense of how amiable God is on account of the beauty of this divine attribute.[21]

Many Christians have a "knowledge" of God and Christ and the doctrines of salvation. But how many have truly "tasted that the Lord is good"? How much of their supposed "knowledge" has any correspondence in their experience? That is the question Edwards was asking. For himself, he knew that "head knowledge," as it is called, was powerless to change the soul. What was needed, and what is needed today, are true Christians who know Christ and his kingdom, not in word only, but in power also. These, like Edwards, will be leaders who change the world for Christ.

HUMILITY

*All gracious affections are broken-hearted
affections.—Jonathan Edwards*

O NE OF THE MOST remarkable aspects of Edwards's character was his humility. From a
purely human perspective, Edwards, of all men, had reason to be proud. He was born with the mind of a genius;
he had the advantage of an early and thorough education;
he was well read; he could write; he could speak in public; he was the product of an aristocratic and well-
connected family; he pastored the most influential church
in his community; and as a result of the Great Awakening,
he was recognized as one of the most powerful preachers
in America.

Yet in spite of these advantages, Edwards had a profound, almost childlike, humility. This humility can be
seen in Edwards's sense of his own sinfulness. As he related in his *Personal Narrative:*

Often, since I live in this town [Northampton], I have had very affecting views of my own sinfulness and vileness; very frequently to such a degree, as to hold me in a kind of loud weeping, sometimes for a considerable time together; so that I have often been forced to shut myself up. I have had a vastly greater sense of my own wickedness, and the badness of my heart, than ever I had before my conversion. It has often appeared to me, that if God should mark iniquity against me, I should appear the very worst of all mankind; of all that have been since the beginning of the world to this time; and that I should have by far the lowest place in hell.[22]

Edwards's growing knowledge of his own wickedness was a sign of his growth in grace. It's not that he was declining in grace, but just the opposite. The more he grew in grace, the more he "saw" his sinfulness and was humbled by it. He continued:

My wickedness, as I am in myself, has long appeared to me perfectly ineffable, and swallowing up all thought and imagination; like an infinite deluge, or mountains over my head. I know not how to express better what my sins appear to me to be, than by heaping infinite upon infinite, and multiplying infinite by infinite. Very often, for these many years, these expressions are in my mind, and in my mouth, "Infinite upon infinite—Infinite upon infinite!" When I look into my heart, and take a view of my wickedness, it looks like an abyss, infinitely deeper than hell. And it appears to me, that were it not for free grace, exalted and raised up to the infinite height of all the fullness and glory of the great Jehovah, and the arm of his power, and in all the glory of his sovereignty, I should appear sunk down in my sins below hell itself; for beyond the sight of every thing, but the eye of sovereign grace, that can pierce even down to such a depth. And yet, it seems to me that my conviction of sin is exceedingly small and faint; it is enough to amaze me, that I have no more sense of my sin. I know certainly, that I have very little sense of my sinfulness. When I have had turns of weeping and crying for my sins, I thought I knew at the time, that my repentance was nothing to my sin.[23]

Edwards's humility before God was not mere emotionalism or "enthusiasm"; it bore the peaceable fruit of meekness before men. For instance, when George Whitefield was touring the colonies, Edwards humbly requested that he visit his church. "I hope it is not wholly from curiosity that I desire to see and hear you in this place; but I apprehend from what I have heard, that you are one that has the blessing of heaven attending you wherever you go; and I have a great desire, if it may be the will of God, that such a blessing as attends your person and labors may descend on this town, and may enter mine own house, and that I may receive it in mine own soul."[24] Edwards then asked Whitefield to remember him in his prayers, yet humbly noted that "I am far from thinking myself worthy to be distinguished" by such remembrance.

When Edwards was asked to take the presidency of Princeton, he declined in a characteristically humble description of himself. One of his chief objections, he said, was "my own defects unfitting me for such an undertaking." What were these defects? According to Edwards: "I have a constitution, in many respects, peculiarly unhappy, attend with flaccid solids, vapid, sizy, and scarce fluids, and a low tide of spirits; often occasioning a kind of childish weakness and contemptibleness of speech, presence and demeanour, with a disagreeable dullness and stiffness, much unfitting me for conversation, but more especially for the government of a college."[25]

That such a description was self-deprecating is evident from the fact that no other similar descriptions are given by Edwards's contemporaries—even his enemies. Indeed, to say of himself that he—one of the great preachers of the Great Awakening—was "contemptible of speech" was nothing short of a miracle of humility.

Many other examples of his humility could be given, but his private reflections reveal the true state of his heart:

> I have greatly longed of late for a broken heart, and to lie low before God; and, when I ask for humility, I cannot bear the thoughts of being no more humble than other Christians. It seems to me, that though their degrees of humility may be suitable for them, yet it would be a vile self-exaltation in me, not to be the lowest in humility of all mankind. Others speak of their longing to be "humbled in the dust"; that may be a proper expression for them, but I always think of myself, that I ought, and it is an expression that has long been natural for me to use in prayer, "to lie infinitely low before God." And its affecting to think, how ignorant I was, when a young Christian, of the bottomless, infinite depths of wickedness, pride, hypocrisy, and deceit, left in my heart.[26]

The sentiments expressed here are foreign to many Christians—both in Edwards's day and in our own—which says much about the insipid state of spirituality among us. If we long to see a new generation of great leaders like Edwards, we must pray for the same spirit of humility that pervaded his life and made him truly great.

HOLINESS

Holiness is a most beautiful, lovely thing.—
Jonathan Edwards

E DWARDS'S SPIRITUALITY EXHIBITED ITSELF not only in a deep humility but also in a profound holiness. All who knew him were impressed with his integrity, honesty, fairness, and modesty, all of which were rooted in his soul's conformity to the will of God.

In one of his earliest sermons, preached to the small congregation in New York that he shepherded for less than a year, Edwards expounded Isaiah 35:8, entitling his sermon "The Way of Holiness." In that sermon he elaborates on a theme that became a hallmark of his preaching and personal life: "It behooves us all to be sensible of the necessity of holiness in order to salvation; of the necessity of real, hearty and sincere, inward and spiritual holiness, such as will stand by us forever and will not leave us at death."[27] In the main section of the sermon, Edwards answers the question "What is holiness?" First, he says, "holiness is a conformity of the heart and life unto God." It is not enough to merely reform one's actions. All outward acts of reformation must proceed from "a most inward, hearty and sincere holiness within." This conformity to God means conformity "to his will, whereby he wills things that are just, right, and truly excellent and lovely; whereby he wills real perfection, and goodness; and perfectly abhors everything that is really evil, unjust, and unreasonable." Moreover, says Edwards, to be holy we must also do "as he doth: in acting holily and justly and wisely and mercifully, like him."

Second, holiness "is a conformity to Jesus Christ." Because Jesus was and is perfectly conformed to God (since he is God), he is the perfect model of holiness. "We have seen his holy life; we have a copy drawn, and an example set for us." Therefore, "holiness is a conformity unto this copy: he that copies after Jesus Christ, after that copy which he has set us and which is delivered to us by the evangelist, is holy."

Third, holiness "is a conformity to God's laws and commands." But again, Edwards is not speaking only, or even primarily, about actions. Rather, this conformity to God's laws must be inward. "When all of God's laws without exception are written in our hearts, then are we holy." And again he says: "If you feel Christ's Sermon upon the Mount engraven on the fleshly tables of our hearts, you are truly sanctified."

At the same time that Edwards was exhorting his flock to seek holiness, he was doing the same in private. His *Personal Narrative* from his New York days shows a passionate longing to possess personal holiness. He wrote:

"My longings after God and holiness were much increased. Pure and humble, holy and heavenly, Christianity appeared exceedingly amiable to me. I felt a burning desire to be, in every thing, a complete Christian; and conformed to the blessed image of Christ."[28]

So great was his desire for personal holiness that he "pursued" and "pressed" after it daily: "It was my continual strife, day and night, and constant inquiry, how I should *be* more holy, and *live* more holily, and more becoming a child of God, and a disciple of Christ. I now sought an increase of grace and holiness, and a holy life, with much more earnestness than ever I sought grace before I had it."

In order to attain holiness, Edwards would severely examine himself daily: "I used to be continually examining myself, and studying and contriving for likely ways and means how I should live holily, with far greater diligence and earnestness than ever I pursued any thing in my life."[29]

It is important to understand that Edwards was not a legalist. Indeed, many confuse the biblical standards of holiness with pharisaical legalism. The two are worlds apart. What Edwards desired was not rules and regulations. Rather, he desired to possess in his soul the reality of heavenly love and purity—the "beauty of holiness," as it is described in Scripture. In fact, it is the beauty or amiableness of holiness that makes Edwards's vision so unlike legalism and so alluring to those who know the ways of God's Spirit.

While in New York, he wrote down his contemplations on holiness: "Holiness . . . appeared to me to be of a sweet, pleasant, a charming, serene, calm nature; which brought an inexpressible purity, brightness, peacefulness, and ravishment to the soul."[30] Edwards's view of holiness is just the opposite of legalism. And although "men are apt to drink in strange notions of holiness from their childhood, as if it were a melancholy, morose, sour and unpleasant thing," on the contrary, it is "sweet and ravishingly lovely."[31]

The beauty of Christianity is the beauty of holiness. And the enduring attraction of Edwards's life and teaching is not his metaphysical subtlety, not his keen intellect, but rather the beauty of his personal holiness.

Duty

> *Resolved to do whatever I think to be my duty and most for the good and advantage of mankind in general. Resolved to do this, whatever difficulties I meet with, how many soever, and how great soever.—Jonathan Edwards*

EDWARDS'S LONG CAREER AS a pastor cannot be properly understood unless we appreciate an important distinction between his day and ours. In Edwards's day, it was common for children to be taught that they had a duty to obey their parents; a duty to serve and worship God; a duty to avoid bad companions; a duty to fulfill the moral law of God as revealed in the Scripture.

Today, of course, we—even those of us in evangelical churches—seldom hear the word *duty* at all. Even in our sermons there seems to be more concern about success, achievement, happiness, victory, etc., than old-fashioned duty. To speak of duty sounds, to our ears, too legalistic, too unfeeling, perhaps even too boring. Yet, for Edwards, duty was the path to true happiness. In his *Personal Narrative,* he observed:

> I had such a sense, how sweet and blessed a thing it was
> to walk in the way of duty; to do that which was right
> and meet to be done, and agreeable to the holy mind of
> God; that it caused me to break forth into a kind of loud
> weeping, which held me some time, so that I was forced
> to shut myself up, and fasten the doors. I could not but,
> as it were, cry out, "How happy are they which do that
> which is right in the sight of God! They are blessed in-
> deed, they are the happy ones!"[32]

Instead of consulting personal pleasure or profit, he
thought in terms of duty to God and man (and always in
that order). As his resolutions show, duty was foremost on
his mind. For instance, ponder Resolution 57: "Resolved,
when I fear misfortunes and adversities, to examine
whether I have done my duty, and resolve, to do it; and
let it be just as Providence orders it, I will, as far as I can,
be concerned about nothing but my duty, and my sin."
Here, Edwards explicitly says he will attempt to focus on
his duty in spite of any adversity he may endure. This, of
course, is the exact opposite of the modern Evangelical
view that if something is difficult or painfu,l it must not be
God's will.

Or consider Resolution 62: "Resolved, never to do any
thing but duty; and then according to Eph. 6:6–8, do it
willingly and cheerfully as unto the Lord, and not to man;
knowing that whatever good thing any man doth, the
same shall he receive of the Lord." Ephesians 6:6–8 is addressed to servants, and they are told to be obedient, "not
with eyeservice, as men-pleasers, but as bondservants of
Christ, doing the will of God from the heart, with good-

will doing service, as to the Lord, and not to men, knowing that whatever good anyone does, he will receive the same from the Lord, whether he is a slave or free" (NKJV).

From his childhood, Edwards exhibited a disposition to duty. As Sereno Dwight noted: "A conscientious regard to duty appeared greatly in the early as well as in the latter days of Jonathan Edwards. As a child, the spirit of love and obedience uniformly guided him; and as a pupil, he discovered [revealed] every disposition honorable to himself, encouraging to those who anxiously watched over his progress, and which was justly considered as the earnest of uncommon attainments."[33]

Not only was he a dutiful son, he was a conscientious and reliable student at Yale, finishing first in his class. When other students rioted over the deplorable food and accommodations, Edwards refused to join them. Moreover, he always strove to fulfill his duty of private devotions, as is clear from his *Resolutions* and *Diary;* and he was a faithful husband and father.

All throughout his ministry, Edwards was animated by his sense of duty to the high calling of the pastorate. He toiled in his study because it was his duty to give his people the best fruits of his research and meditation. In fact, he preached on subjects that many pastors refused to address—the heinousness of sin, the awful judgment of God, and the horrible reality of hell—because he believed that it was his duty to be God's spokesman regardless of the subject and regardless of the outcome. If Edwards believed the Bible taught a particular doctrine, then he felt morally bound to proclaim it, whether his people liked it or not.

The most clear example of Edwards's dedication to duty can be seen in his willingness during the communion controversy to sacrifice his position for the sake of principle. As Samuel Hopkins summed up the matter:

> Mr. Edwards had a numerous and chargeable family, and little or no income, exclusive of his salary; and, considering how far he was advanced in years; the general disposition of people, who want a minister, to prefer a young man who has never been settled, to one who has been dismissed from his people; and what misrepresentations were made of his principles through the country, it looked to him not at all probable that he should ever have opportunity to be settled again in the work of the ministry, if he was dismissed from Northampton: and he was not inclined or able to take any other course, or go into any other business to get a living: so that beggary as well as disgrace stared him full in the face, if he persisted in his principles. When he was fixed in his principles, and before they were publicly known, he told some of his friends, that if he discovered [revealed] and persisted in them, it would most likely issue in his dismission and disgrace; and the ruin of himself and family, as to their *temporal interests.* He therefore first sat down and counted the cost, and deliberately took up the cross, when it was set before him in its full weight and magnitude; and in direct opposition to all *worldly* views and motives. And therefore his conduct in these circumstances, was a remarkable exercise and discovery of his conscientiousness; and his readiness to deny himself, and forsake all that he had, to follow Christ. A man must have a considerable

degree of the spirit of a martyr, to go on with the stead-fastness and resolution with which he did. He ventured wherever truth and duty appeared to lead him, unmoved at the threatening dangers on every side.[34]

Duty called and Edwards obeyed. There is no higher example of Christlike leadership.

Love for God

Thus love would dispose to all duties, both toward
God and toward man.—Jonathan Edwards

T HERE IS AN UNFORTUNATE perception that Edwards was a stern, even austere, man. This perception is due to several factors. First, he was temperamentally shy; some even would say unsociable. Second, Edwards was not afraid to preach the hard truths of the Bible, such as sin, judgment, and hell. Third, when his works were first gathered and unpublished, more space was given to his theoretical works than to his sermons, and the sermons chosen for publication happened to be those that dwelled on "hard truths." Thus, for many years, the only picture of Edwards that many people knew was drawn from an early edition of his collected works.

But much of what he preached and wrote was left out of those early editions. And one set of sermons in particular, which might have changed his image, was a series of sermons he gave on 1 Corinthians 13—the "Love Chapter" as it has been called. These were not published until 1852 under the title *Charity and Its Fruits*. These sermons were given in Northampton in 1738, as the first revival in his church began to subside. It shows not only a bright mind, but a man with a large and tender heart. Space, of course, limits us to touch on only the theme of these sixteen sermons.

According to Edwards, love, or charity as it was then often called, was the hallmark of the true Christian. The doctrine of the opening sermon is this: "That all the virtue that is saving, and that distinguishes true Christians from others, is summed up in Christian love."[35] Note that Edwards highlighted the fact that only the "saved" truly have love; thus love is the chief mark of genuine conversion. Here Edwards echoes one of his constant concerns; that is, how to discern true from false conversion. Coming at the close of a revival, there is no doubt that Edwards intended these sermons to be used by his new converts as a tool for self-examination.

Edwards first argues this doctrine from reason. He says first, "That love will dispose to all proper and of respect to both God and man. This is evident, because a true respect for either God or man *consists* in love. If a man sincerely loves God, it will dispose him to render all proper respect to him; and men need no other incitement to shew each other all the respect that is due, than love."[36]

Though the following explanation is long, it is worth quoting in full in order to appreciate Edwards's vision of what it means to love God:

Love to God will dispose a man to honour him, to worship and adore him, and heartily to acknowledge his
greatness and glory and dominion. And so it will dispose
to all acts of obedience to God; for the servant that loves
his master, and the subject that loves his sovereign, will
be disposed to proper subjection and obedience. Love
will dispose that Christian to behave toward God, as a
child to a father; amid difficulties, to resort to him for
help, and put all his trust in him; just as it is natural for
us, in case of need of affliction, to go to one that we love
for pity and help. It will lead us, too, to give credit to his
word, and to put confidence in him; for we are not apt to
suspect the veracity of those we have entire friendship
for. It will dispose us to praise God for the mercies we receive from him, just as we are disposed to gratitude for
any kindness we receive from our fellow-men that we
love. Love, again, will dispose our hearts to submission to
the will of God, for we are more willing that the will of
those we love should be done, than of others. We naturally desire that those we love should be suited, and that
we should be agreeable to them; and true affection and
love to God will dispose the heart to acknowledge God's
right to govern, and that he is worthy to do it, and so will
dispose to submission. Love to God will dispose us to
walk humbly with him, for he that loves God will be disposed to acknowledge the vast distance between God
and himself. It will be agreeable to such an one, to exalt
God, and set him on high above all, to lie low before him.
A true Christian delights to have God exalted on his own
abasement, because he loves him. He is willing to own
that God is worthy of this, and it is with delight that he

casts himself in the dust before the Most High, from his sincere love to him.[37]

Men and women who love God, as that love is described by Edwards, are the kind of leaders needed in our day.

LOVE FOR MAN

Resolved, to be endeavouring to find out fit objects of liberality and charity.—Jonathan Edwards

DWARDS'S VIEW OF LOVE also included love for our neighbor. Indeed, love for God and love for man were, in his view, inseparable. In *Charity and Its Fruits,* Edwards says, "A due consideration of the nature of love will shew that it disposes men to all duties toward their neighbours."[38] This means that men will act justly, truthfully, and humbly. It will cause men to "honour one another," to be content and not to covet, and "it will dispose men to meekness and gentleness in their carriage toward their neighbours." Addressing the besetting sin of the town of Northampton, Edwards says that love "will check and restrain everything like a bitter spirit; for love has no bitterness in it, but is a gentle and sweet disposition and affection of the soul. It will prevent broils and quarrels, and will dispose men to peaceableness, and to forgive injurious treatment received from others."[39]

Moreover, according to Edwards, "love will dispose to all acts of mercy" and will incline men to "give to the poor, to bear one another's burdens, and to weep with those that weep." Love will also govern men in their several "places and relations." In other words, love will cause us to fulfill our duties to our rulers, our ministers, our parents, and our masters.[40] Love, says Edwards, "is a principle which, if it be implanted in the heart, is alone sufficient to produce all good practice; and every right disposition toward God and man is summed up in it, and comes from it, as the fruit from the tree, or the stream from the fountain."[41] This love is "the sum of all . . . contained in the law of God, and of all duties required in his word." The first table shows us our duties toward God; the second table, toward man. Love fulfills both; for, as the apostle Paul has said, "Love is the fulfilling of the law" (Romans 13:10).

For Edwards, the important thing about love is that it "is an ingredient in true and living faith, and is what is most essential and distinguishing in it."[42] In other words, if there is no true love, there is no true and saving faith: "A speculative faith consists only in the assent of the understanding; but in a saving faith there is also the consent of the heart." To believe without love is to have the "faith of the devils." As in his many works on revival, Edwards was again inviting his listeners to examine themselves to see if they were truly converted.

Edwards expected love to manifest itself in life, and one key was benevolence or almsgiving. Thus he taught his church to be "much in deeds of charity." As he said in a 1741 sermon, during the height of the revival in Northampton:

The way of the practice of all duty is the way in which persons should seek the grace of God, and especially the more important duties. But this duty of charity to the poor is in God's account a very important duty, as appears by its being so much insisted on in the Word of God. 'Tis more important than outward act of worship, as appears by Matt. 9:13, "I will have mercy, and not sacrifice." God has appointed this as a way wherein we should seek his grace: from his goodness. The duty of charity or almsgiving is in a peculiar manner agreeable to the attribute of his goodness and, therefore, he especially encourages persons to seek him in this way.[43]

Edwards modeled this kind of love for his fellow man for his congregation. He demonstrated, noted Samuel Hopkins, "great benevolence to mankind" by the concern he showed for the poor and distressed. He recommended charity in both his public and private conversation. He saw that his church maintained a fund for the poor to be administered by the deacons. He regularly supported public charity, such as Whitefield's orphanage in Georgia. Moreover, he was quick to privately relieve suffering and made it a point to conceal his generosity as much as possible.[44]

Much of the success of Edwards's ministry can probably be attributed to the fact that he genuinely loved his family, his friends, and his neighbors. Talk is cheap; love is not. It is the evidence of sincerity—a sure sign of a man's integrity. Men follow character, not words. And Edwards swayed others not only by the power of his intellect but also by the power of his love.

MINISTRY

May God bless you with a faithful pastor, one that is well acquainted with his mind and will, thoroughly warning sinners, wisely and skillfully searching professors, and conducting you in the way to eternal blessedness.—Jonathan Edwards

*A*s I noted before, Edwards's lasting fame is probably due more to his philosophical and theological treatises than anything else. They are remarkable indeed. But although he had a speculative and philosophical bent of mind, Edwards surrendered his intellect to the main calling of his life—the ministry.

Fortunately, Edwards recorded his views on the ministry. At various times he was asked to preach at churches outside Northampton, one of which was the ordination of a new minister. On August 30, 1744, he was invited to Pelham to preach at the ordination of Robert Abercrombie. Edwards's sermon, titled "The True Excellency of a Gospel Minister," was based on John 5:35, where Jesus commends John the Baptist as an example to ministers. His doctrine or subject was this: "It is the excellency of a minister of the gospel to be both a burning and a shining light."[45]

First, a minister of the gospel is to give light. And in Scripture, light has a threefold use: "to discover [reveal], to refresh, and to direct." Thus, "ministers are set to be lights to the souls of men in this respect, as they are to be the means of imparting divine truth to them, and bringing into their view the most glorious and excellent objects, and of leading them to, and assisting them in the contemplation of those things that angels desire to look into. . . . They are set to be the means of bringing them out of darkness into God's marvelous light, and of bringing them to the infinite fountain of light . . . they are set to instruct men, and impart to them that knowledge by which they may know God and Jesus Christ, whom to know is life eternal."

But light also refreshes. So "ministers are set in the church of God to be the instruments of this comfort and refreshment to the souls of men, to be the instruments of leading souls to the God of all consolation, and fountain of their happiness." They are "to preach good tidings to the meek, to bind up the broken hearted, to proclaim liberty to the captives, and the opening of the prison to them that are bound, and to comfort all that mourn."

Third, ministers use light to direct, since "'tis by light that we see where to go . . . 'tis by light men see what to do and are enabled to work." Thus, "ministers have the record of God committed to them that they may hold that forth, which God has given to be to man as a light shining in a dark place, to guide them in the way through this dark world, to regions of eternal light." Ministers, therefore, "are set to be instruments of conveying to men that true wisdom" of God.

In order for a minister to fulfill his calling of giving light, he must himself be a burning and shining light. What does this mean?

First, he must be a *burning* light. He must have a heart that is "full of much of the holy ardor of a spirit of true piety." The power of godliness, says Edwards, "is no dull, inactive, ineffectual principle; it is a powerful thing; there is an exceeding energy in it; and the reason is, that God is in it; it is a driving principle; a participation of the divine nature, a communication of the divine life." Therefore, a minister who is a burning light has "his soul enkindled with the heavenly flame; his heart burns with love to Christ, and fervent desires of the advancement of his kingdom and glory; and also with ardent love to the souls of men, and desires for their salvation." And this burning or holy ardor will manifest itself in all that a minister does: he will be "zealous and fervent in his administrations." Thus, his fervent zeal "appears in the fervency of his prayers to God, for and with his people; and in the earnestness and power with which he preaches the word of God . . . ; and the unfeigned earnestness and compassion with which he invites the weary and heavy laden to their Saviour . . . ; comforts and counsels the saints . . . ; and maintains the exercise of discipline in the house of God."

In addition, a minister must be a *shining* light. He must, first, "be pure, clear, and full in his doctrine." He must be "able to teach, not a novice, or one unskillful in the word of righteousness." Thus, he "must be one that is well studied in divinity, well acquainted with the written word of God, mighty in the Scriptures, and able to instruct and convince gainsayers." He must be "diligent in teaching" and "careful and faithful to declare the whole counsel of God."

He must also, in order to shine, "be discreet in all his administrations." This means that his zeal must be tempered with wisdom, and he must "know how to conduct himself in the house of God, as a wise builder, and a wise steward." But he must also shine "in his conversation." His conduct must confirm his message. He must let his light shine by his good works. "God sent his Son into the world to be the light of the world these two ways, viz., by revealing his mind and will to the world, and also by setting [for] the world a perfect example." So ministers are to do likewise.

In order to fulfill their calling, Edwards gives ministers the following advice. First, they "should be diligent in their studies, and in the work of the ministry . . . ; giving themselves wholly to it . . . giving up the profits and vainglory of the world." Second, they must be "very conversant with the holy Scriptures; making it very much their business, with the utmost diligence and strictness, to search those holy writings."

More important, ministers must "seek after much of the spiritual knowledge of Christ, and that they may live in the clear view of his glory." It is not enough to know about Christ from the Word. Ministers must know him in a personal and deep way. For "by this means they will be changed into the image of the same glory and brightness, and will come to their people as Moses came down to the congregation of Israel." And last, ministers must "walk closely with God, and keep near Christ." This requires that "they should be much in seeking God, and conversing with him by prayer." As little children, they should sit "at Christ's feet to hear his word, and be instructed by him."

That Edwards practiced what he preached is without question. For, as Dr. Samuel Finley said of him: "Among the luminaries of the church, in these American regions, he was justly reputed a star of the first magnitude."[46] Edwards himself was a burning and shining light.

CHRISTLIKENESS

Christ, as he is a divine person, is the Lord of heaven and earth, and so one of infinite dignity, to whom our supreme respect is due; and on that account he is infinitely worthy that we should regard, not only his precepts, but example. The infinite honorableness of his person recommends his virtues, and a conformity to them as our greatest dignity and honor.—Jonathan Edwards

WHEREAS IN FORMER SERMONS Edwards commended John the Baptist as an honorable example for ministers, in a sermon given five years later, at the ordination of Job Strong on June 28, 1749, Edwards held up Christ as the ultimate example for those who aspire to leadership in the church. His text was John 13:15–16, and his thesis was "that it is the duty of ministers of the gospel, in the work of their ministry, to follow the example of their great Lord and Master."[47]

Most important, ministers (and likewise all Christian leaders) "should follow their Lord and Master in all those excellent virtues, and in that universal and eminent holiness of life, which he set an example of in his human nature." Edwards elaborated:

> The ministers of Christ should be persons of the same spirit that their Lord was of: the same spirit of humility and lowliness of heart; for the servant is not greater than his Lord. They should be of the same spirit of heavenly-mindedness and contempt of the glory, wealth and pleasures of this world: they should be of the same spirit of devotion and fervent love to God: they should follow the example of his prayerfulness. . . .

But Edwards did not stop there. There was more— much more:

> Ministers should follow Christ's example, in his strict, constant and inflexible observance of the commands which God had given him, touching what he should do and what he should say; he spake nothing of himself, but those things which the Father had commanded him, those he spake, and always did those things that pleased him, and continued in thorough obedience in the greatest trials, and through the greatest opposition that ever there was any instance of. Ministers should be persons of the same quiet, lamb-like spirit that Christ was of, the same spirit of submission to God's will, and patience under afflictions, and meekness towards men, of the same calmness and composure of spirit under reproaches and suffering from the malignity of evil men; of the same spirit of

forgiveness of injuries; of the same spirit of charity, of
fervent love and extensive benevolence; the same disposition to pity the miserable, to weep with those that
weep, to help men under their calamities of both soul
and body, to hear and grant the requests of the needy,
and relieve the afflicted; the same spirit of condescen-
sion to the poor and mean, tenderness and gentleness
towards the weak, and great and effectual love to enemies. They should also be of the same spirit of zeal,
diligence and self-denial for the glory of God, and the
advancement of his kingdom, and for the good of
mankind; for which things' sake Christ went through
the greatest labors, and endured the most extreme suf-
ferings.

The example of Christ is an example not only for
ministers. He is *the* example for *all* Christians, and he is
especially the example for all Christian leaders. Indeed,
Christian leadership, by its very definition, should differ
from secular leadership in this regard: a Christian leader
must conform his life and his leadership to Christ.
There is only one moral standard for Christians,
whether they be in business, medicine, law, politics, or
church: Jesus Christ.

How, then, can we become Christlike leaders? Edwards's simple answer is that we should spend time with
Jesus: "That we may *be* and *behave* like Christ, we should
earnestly seek much acquaintance with him, and much
love to him, and be much in secret converse with him." By
a natural law, we become like those we spend time with:
"It is natural, and as it were necessary for us to imitate

those whom we are much acquainted and conversant with, and have a strong affection for."

We may say the standard is too high. But it is we who must change, not the standard. To lead like Christ, spend time with Christ. There is no other way to Christlike leadership.

CIVIC LEADERSHIP

*Almost all the prosperity of a public society and
civil community does, under God, depend on
their rulers.—Jonathan Edwards*

*A*S WE HAVE SEEN, Edwards's ministry in Northampton was marked for years by conflict.
He was resisted by a group within the community who
had Arminian leanings. However, due to the influence of
John Stoddard, who was a member of the king's council
and the leading citizen in town, Edwards was shielded
from open resistance. Stoddard was a model magistrate
whose leadership had a wholesome and unifying influence on the town.

When Stoddard died in June 1748, Edwards gave the
funeral oration and revealed his views on civil leadership.
Using as his text Ezekiel 19:12 ("Her strong rods were
broken and withered"), Edwards expounded the following subject: "When God by death removes from a people
those in place of public authority and rule that have been

as strong rods, it is an awful judgment of God on that people, and worthy of great lamentation."[48]

Edwards highlighted the qualities needed in a good ruler. First, a good ruler must have "great ability for the management of public affairs." This "great ability" involves an "uncommon strength of reason and largeness of understanding," especially "a genius for government, a peculiar turn of mind fitting them to gain an extraordinary understanding in things of that nature." Civic leaders must likewise have "an extraordinary talent for distinguishing what is right and just . . . to see through the false colors with which injustice is often disguised." They must also have "a great knowledge of human nature, and of the way of accommodating themselves to it, so as most effectually to influence it to wise purposes." Good rulers must possess an extensive knowledge of "the state and circumstance of the country of people that they have the care of, and know well their laws and constitution, and what their circumstances require" as well as knowledge of "neighbor nations, states, or providences."

Second, civil leaders must possess "largeness of heart, and a greatness and nobleness of disposition." Edwards elaborates: "One that abhors those things that are mean and sordid, and not capable of a compliance with them; one that is of a public spirit, and not of a private, narrow disposition; a man of honor, and not a man of mean artifice and clandestine management, for filthy lucre, and one that abhors trifling and impertinence, or to waste away his time, that should be spent in the service of God, his king, or his country, in vain amusements and diversions, and in the pursuit of the gratifications of sensual appetites."

Third, good public leaders are endowed with "much of a spirit of government," which means not only a knowledge of government but also a talent for applying that knowledge in particular situations. It also means "eminent fortitude," or courage, and a "spirit of resolution and activity, so as to keep the wheels of government in proper motion, and to cause judgment and justice to run down as a mighty stream."

Fourth, magistrates must be people of personal virtue; or, as Edwards articulated it, they must have "stability and firmness of integrity, fidelity, and piety." By their "strict integrity and righteousness," civil rulers are firm in executing justice and in suppressing "vice and immorality." They will influence by personal example, be faithful to their public trust, and will not "follow the multitude" or advance their "private interest."

Last, Edwards mentions the advantages of education, reputation, "forcible speech," and the rulers' "good presence, majesty of countenance, decency of behavior."

The blessings that flow from godly civil authorities are innumerable, and Edwards summarized a few:

> The prosperity of a people depends more on their rulers than is commonly imagined. . . . Their influence has a tendency to promote their wealth, and cause their temporal possessions and blessing to abound: and to promote virtue amongst them, and so to unite them one to another in peace and mutual benevolence, and make them happy in society; and by these means to advance their reputation and honor in the world; and which is much more, to promote their spiritual and eternal happiness.

Edwards was right to say that such rulers are "great gifts of the Most High to a people." And Christians who serve in the civil sphere are called to be such leaders.

PREACHING

They [ministers] should imitate the faithfulness of
Christ in his ministry, in speaking whatsoever God
had commanded him, and declaring the whole
counsel of God.—Jonathan Edwards

*M*ANY SCHOLARS, ENAMORED OF Edwards's
acute intellect, forget that his main business, his life work, was preaching. All of the ideas that
were later developed in his larger theological treatises can
be found in his sermons. His sermons were Edwards's "fa-
vored literary form and his most time-consuming activity."[49] As pastor, he regularly preached two hour-long
sermons on Sunday and gave midweek lectures, not to
mention preaching at other churches on special occasions.
During the Great Awakening, Edwards preached daily.

Yet it is striking that Edwards was not a "great
preacher" in the popular sense. He was not, for instance,
a pulpiteer or orator like George Whitefield. Though
Whitefield was profoundly sincere in his preaching, he
had a flare for the dramatic. His voice was mellifluous, his
eye aflame, his gestures theatrical. In fact, he was the

envy of the British stage. Edwards, on the other hand, was the opposite. He had a mild though clear voice. He often read his sermons from a manuscript. He seldom gestured. Some said he stared at a bell rope in the back of the church (but how he could do this while reading a manuscript is unclear).

Secular historians and sociologists, who have no personal experience of God's Spirit or genuine revival, have assumed that Edwards would rant and rave in his preaching; that is how they "explain" the impact of his preaching. But Edwards was the polar opposite of the stereotypical "revivalist" preacher—screaming and hollering, thumping his Bible, and strutting across the stage. If anything, his pulpit delivery was plain and modest. From a human perspective, the effect of his sermons was, and is, inexplicable. As Sereno Dwight described it: "In his preaching, usually all was plain, familiar, sententious, and practical."[50] The form of his sermons was standard for the time: exposition, doctrine (with development), and application. Occasionally he deviated from this pattern, but not often.

The impact of Edwards's preaching was often remarkable. Dr. Stephen West, of Stockbridge, recalled on one occasion that Edwards preached for two hours while the audience was "fixed and motionless." They seemed disappointed that he did not continue the sermon longer.[51] Dr. Benjamin Trumbull related that Edwards preached at Enfield, and when the people gathered in the church they "were thoughtless and vain. The people hardly conducted themselves with common decency." But by the time Edwards's sermon had concluded, they were "deeply impressed, and bowed down with an awful conviction of their sin and danger."[52]

The value and success of Edwards's preaching lay, first of all, in the depth of his subject matter. He was a didactic preacher. His sermons were full of Bible and theological teachings. He was considered one of the most learned preachers of his day. He also had a profound knowledge of the human heart, which was the result of both his study of the Scripture and his spiritual exercises in private devotions. He often practiced self-examination, which gave him keen insight into the depths of the human soul.

Edwards had also a "deep and pervading solemnity" of mind that was striking and impressive to his audience. The doctrines he preached seemed "real" to him—he could "see," it seems, the glories of heaven and the miseries of hell. His sense of an ever-present God was a weighty influence on his hearers. And although Edwards was not a demonstrative preacher, his feelings were nevertheless intense. As Samuel Hopkins observed: "His words often discovered a great degree of inward fervour, without much noise or external emotion, and fell with great weight on the minds of his hearers."[53]

When Edwards's biographer, Sereno Dwight, asked Dr. West (who had often heard Edwards preach) if Edwards was an *eloquent* preacher, he replied:

> If you mean, by eloquence, what is usually intended by it in our cities; he had no pretensions to it. He had no studied varieties of the voice, and no strong emphasis. He scarcely gestured, or even moved; and he made no attempt, by the elegance of his style, or the beauty of his

pictures, to gratify the taste, and fascinate the imagination. But if you mean by eloquence, the power of present-
ing an important truth before an audience, with an
overwhelming weight of argument, and with such in-
tenseness of feeling, that the whole soul of the speaker is
thrown into every part of the conception and delivery; so
that the solemn attention of the whole audience is riv-
eted, from the beginning to the close, and impressions are
left that cannot be effaced; Mr. Edwards was the most
eloquent man I ever heard.[54]

FAMILY

Every Christian family ought to be as it were a little church, consecrated to Christ, and wholly influenced and governed by his rules.—Jonathan Edwards

EDWARDS'S COMMITMENT TO GOD and his church did not cause him, like some pastors, to lose touch with his family. He had an "uncommon union" with his beloved Sarah, and he was a dutiful father to his many children.

His concern for biblical family government is seen in his farewell sermon, where he gives his former flock one last exhortation to regulate their families according to the Scriptures:

One thing that greatly concerns you, as you would be a happy people, is the maintaining of *family order.* . . . Every Christian family ought to be as it were a little church, consecrated to Christ, and wholly influenced and governed by his rules. And family education and order are some of the chief of the means of grace. If these fail, all other means are likely to prove ineffectual. If these are duly maintained, all the means of grace will be likely to prosper and be successful.[55]

To the parents or "heads of families," Edwards urged:

To great painfulness, in teaching, warning, and directing their children; bringing them up in the nurture and admonition of the Lord; beginning early, when there is yet opportunity, and maintaining a constant diligence in labors of this kind; remembering that, as you would not have all your instructions and counsels ineffectual, there must be government as well as instructions, which must be maintained with an even hand, and steady resolution, as guard to the religion and morals of the family, and the support of good order. Take heed that it be not with any of you as with Eli of old, who reproved his children but restrained them not; and that, by this means, you do not bring the like curse on your families as he did on his.[56]

To the children, for whom Edwards had a great love, he said:

And let children obey their parents, and yield to their instructions, and submit to their orders, as they would inherit a blessing and not a curse. For we have reason to think, from many things in the word of God, that nothing has greater tendency to bring a curse on persons in this world, and on all their temporal concerns, than an undutiful, unsubmissive, disorderly behavior in children towards their parents.[57]

From the testimony we have of those who knew Edwards, he happily practiced what he preached. He had a good relationship with his wife, which is the fountain of a happy and orderly home. They prayed together daily in his study, usually before bedtime.

He governed his family firmly but not harshly. He seldom needed to use corporal punishment but could usually bring his children into submission by his authority, reason, and the Word of God. According to Samuel Hopkins, "He kept a watchful eye over his children, that he might admonish them of the first wrong step, and direct them in the right way."[58] He often prayed with his children and taught them the Scriptures and the Westminster Shorter Catechism. Edwards was likewise watchful of his children's friendships. He rarely allowed his children to "hang out" with young people because he saw it as "a dangerous step towards corrupting and bringing them to ruin."[59] And he likewise maintained an early curfew of nine o'clock in the evening.

It is sad but often true that good men have bad children. But this was not the case with Edwards. His children, trained under his loving and careful eye, were a testimony to the grace of God and their father's love as well as a testimony to his sound leadership.

Spiritual Disciplines

This day, [I was] revived by God's Holy Spirit.—
Jonathan Edwards

*E*DWARDS'S GREAT SPIRITUALITY WAS born of his commitment to the spiritual disciplines of meditation, prayer, and fasting. As we have seen, he was a devoted student of the Scriptures. Yet his interest in the Word was not just intellectual; it was also spiritual. Edwards sought not only knowledge of the Word but also knowledge of the Living Word—Christ himself.

In addition to the study of, and meditation upon, the Word, Edwards also devoted himself to the disciplines of fasting and prayer. As Samuel Hopkins observed:

He who enters into the true spirit of our author's writings, and especially of the extracts we have given from his private papers, cannot question that he made conscience of private devotion; but, as he made a secret of such exercises, nothing can be said of them but what his papers discover, and what may be fairly inferred from circumstances. It appears, by his Diary, that in his youth he determined to attend secret prayer more than twice a day, when circumstances would allow; and there is much evidence that he was frequent and punctual in that duty, often kept days of fasting and prayer, and set apart portions of time for devout meditations on spiritual and eternal things, as part of his religious exercise in retirement.[60]

Biographer Sereno Dwight amplified Hopkins's reflections:

The habits of his religious life . . . were thorough and exact. His observation of the Sabbath was such as to make it, throughout, a day of real religion; so that not only were his conversation and reading conformed to the great design of the day, but he allowed himself in no thoughts or meditations, which were not decidedly of a religious character. It was his rule, not only to search the Scriptures daily, but to study them so steadily, constantly, and frequently, as that he might perceive a regular and obvious growth in his knowledge of them. By prayer and self-application, he took constant care to render them the means of progressive sanctification. . . . There is much evidence that he was punctual, constant, and frequent in secret prayer, and often kept days of fasting and prayer in secret, and set apart time for serious, devout meditation on spiritual and eternal things, as part of his religious exercises in secret. . . . He was, as far as can be known, much on his knees in secret, and in devout reading of God's Word, and meditation upon it.[61]

While Edwards spent hours in meditation, prayer, and fasting for his own spiritual benefit, he also spent much time praying and fasting for others and for the advancement of Christ's kingdom. As he exhorted his fellow ministers in an ordination sermon:

> Ministers should be animated in this work by a great love to the souls of men, and should be ready to spend and be spent for them; for Christ loved them, and gave himself for them: he loved them with a love stronger than death. They should have compassion to men under their spiritual miseries, as Christ had pity on them. They should be much in prayer for the people of their flock, considering how Christ prayed and agonized for them, in tears of blood. They should travail in birth with the souls that are committed to their care, seeing their own salvation is the fruit of the travail of Christ's soul.[62]

Edwards was confident that prayer and fasting were a key means of spiritual awakening, revival, and advancement of the kingdom. Writing in defense of the awakening in New England, Edwards encouraged all concerned to prayer and fasting:

> So is God's will, through this wonderful grace, that the prayers of his saints should be one great and principal means of carrying on the designs of Christ's kingdom in the world. When God has something very great to accomplish for his church, it is his will, that there should precede it, the extraordinary prayers of his people; as is manifest by Ezek. xxxvi. 37, "I will yet, for this, be inquired of, by the

house of Israel, to do it for them"; together with the context. And it is revealed that, when God is about to accomplish great things for his church, he will begin by remarkably pouring out the Spirit of grace and supplication. Zech. xii. 10. If we are not to expect the devil should go out of a particular person, that is under bodily possession, without extraordinary prayer, or *prayer and fasting;* how much less should we expect to have him cast out of the land and the world without it.[63]

Indeed, Edwards not only participated in the concert of prayer, but he wrote a significant treatise vigorously promoting prayer and fasting as the means to advancing the kingdom. As he articulated it in *A Humble Attempt:* "From the whole we may infer, that it is a very *suitable* thing, and *well-pleasing to God,* for many people, in different parts of the world, by express *agreement,* to come into a *visible union,* in extraordinary, speedy, fervent and constant *prayer,* for those great effusions of the *Holy Spirit,* which shall bring on the *advancement* of Christ's church and kingdom, that God has so often promised shall be in the *latter ages* of the world."[64]

Though all Christian leaders ought to practice spiritual disciplines, it is especially incumbent on spiritual leaders to practice them, not only for personal growth, but so that the Spirit of God may rest on their labors.

EXPERIENTIAL RELIGION

There is no question whatsoever, that is of greater importance to mankind, and that it more concerns every individual person to be well resolved in than this: What are the distinguishing qualifications of those that are in favor with God, and entitled to his eternal rewards?—Jonathan Edwards

IN ORDER TO ANSWER this question, Edwards penned the classic work *A Treatise Concerning Religious Affections*. It was more than a defense of revival. It was an exploration and explanation of God's gracious operations in the soul. It was an apology for vital godliness over against a dead orthodoxy. And moreover, it was an instrument for self-examination.

Edwards does admit that the Great Awakening contained a "mixture of counterfeit religion with true," and that "the devil has had his greatest advantage against the cause and kingdom of Christ all along hitherto." It was precisely because this mixture had caused such confusion that Edwards felt the need to address the issue.

In summary, Edwards discriminated between "false and gracious affections" and between affections and "passions." The latter are dark emotions that hinder the formation of "gracious affections." Edwards then identified love as the controlling affection. He demonstrated from the Scriptures the large part that affections played in the lives of eminent saints.

Edwards then described those signs that indicate false affections. Or, to put it differently, he argued that certain "signs" such as bodily effects, fervor, zeal, praise, moving testimonies, and others do not necessarily prove a genuine work of the Spirit. Edwards was strongly skeptical that a mere religious activity such as reading, praying, or singing is a sign of true godly affections. By themselves, these "signs" are no guarantee of saving grace.

In the third and largest part of *Religious Affections,* Edwards offered a detailed description of twelve signs of "truly gracious and holy affections." They are:

1. Gracious Affections are from Divine Influence
2. Their Object is the Excellence of Divine Things
3. They are founded on the moral Excellency of Objects
4. They arise from Divine Illumination
5. They are attended with a Conviction of Certainty
6. They are attended with Evangelical Humiliation
7. They are attended with a Change of Nature
8. They beget and promote the Temper of Jesus
9. Gracious Affections soften the Heart
10. They have beautiful Symmetry and Proportion
11. False Affections rest satisfied in Themselves

12. Religious Affections have their fruit in Christian Practice

While space does not permit a thorough analysis of these signs, it is important to note a few features of Edwards's exposition.

First, he avoided the false dichotomy between "head and heart." The affections are not emotions; they are inclinations of the will in response to the mind. Although emotions are involved, true religious affections are rooted in a divinely enlightened mind. Thus, he was not advocating "emotionalism" as we use that term today.

Second, Edwards distanced himself from the fanatical fringe of the Great Awakening by pointing out that true religion reveals itself in virtues like "evangelical humiliation" and "the temper of Jesus." Nothing was more repugnant to Edwards than the pride and arrogance of enthusiasts like James Davenport. What is missing from their experience is humility, a sense of sin, and true repentance. "All gracious affections are broken-hearted affections," Edwards argued.[65] And true saints are "those that do mourn" for their sins.[66]

Third, it is obvious from Edwards's treatment of the affections that he believed the crucial test of any spiritual experience was a life of holiness. When the Holy Spirit abides in the soul, he imparts to it his own special property of holiness. A convert, therefore, will demonstrate a permanent change of "temper." He will now be inclined away from evil and toward good. For a true saint, holiness is "the most amiable and sweet thing that is to be found in heaven or earth."[67] He will be grieved at his remaining corruption and strive after holiness. He will resolve to live a life of obedience to God.

That is perhaps the most important point to be made on the subject. Over and over again, Edwards hammered away at the fallacy of cheap grace. Affections are an important part of true religion, but if the life is not changed—and changed in the direction of holiness—then the affections are false and the religion is vain.

SOVEREIGNTY

I had, at that same time, a very affecting sense, how meet and suitable it was that God should govern the world, and order all things according to his own pleasure; and I rejoiced in it, that God reigned, and that his will was done.—Jonathan Edwards

*W*HEN EDWARDS WAS INVITED to give the Thursday lecture in Boston in July 1731, he gave his now-famous sermon "God Glorified in Man's Dependence." Some of the leading citizens were so impressed that they begged Edwards's permission to print the sermon. Published in August of that year, the original title read: *God Glorified in the Work of Redemption, by the Greatness of Man's Dependence Upon Him in the Whole of It.*

The theme of the sermon, of course, was God's sovereignty in the salvation of man. And this theme became in some ways central to much of Edwards's subsequent preaching and writing. From this time on, he was seen as a champion of God's sovereignty.

It may be surprising to learn that Edwards did not always embrace the notion of God's sovereignty. He tells us in his *Personal Narrative:* "From my childhood up, my mind had been wont to be full of objections against the doctrine of God's sovereignty, in choosing whom he would to eternal life, and rejecting whom he pleased; leaving them eternally to perish, and be everlastingly tormented in hell. It used to appear like a horrible doctrine to me."[68]

Yet somehow (Edwards doesn't seem to know how) he came to accept this "horrible doctrine":

> But I remember the time very well, when I seemed to be convinced, and fully satisfied, as to this sovereignty of God, and his justice in thus eternally disposing of men, according to his sovereign pleasure. But never could give an account, how, or by what means, I was thus convinced; not in the least imagining, in the time of it, nor a long time after, that there was any extraordinary influence of God's Spirit in it: but only that now I saw further, and my reason apprehended the justice and reasonableness of it.[69]

Not only did Edwards acquiesce to this doctrine, he came to fully embrace it—to *delight* in it. He continued:

> God's absolute sovereignty, and justice, with respect to salvation and damnation, is what my mind seems to rest assured of, as much as of anything that I see with my eyes; at least it is so at times. But I have oftentimes since that first conviction, had quite another kind of sense of

God's sovereignty, that I had then. I have often since, not only had a conviction, but a *delightful* conviction. The doctrine of God's sovereignty has very often appeared, an exceeding pleasant, bright and sweet doctrine to me: and absolute sovereignty is what I love to ascribe to God.[70]

It seems puzzling that someone generally so aware of his own spiritual struggles and development should be at a loss to know how he came to accept God's sovereignty. Despite Edwards's uncertainty, I would venture this possible explanation. First, Edwards was a serious student of the Bible, and whatever objections he initially had, his study of the Scriptures must have removed them. It is clear that he did not accept sovereignty, or any other doctrine, on merely human authority. Edwards was addicted to sorting out problems (usually on paper) for himself. He was not about to embrace this doctrine just because his father did or because Solomon Stoddard did. He "called no man father." So we can only assume that his intense study of the Bible convinced him that the doctrine of God's absolute sovereignty was a *divine* doctrine, not the invention of men. In a sermon titled "God's Sovereignty," he marshaled numerous biblical texts to support this doctrine.[71]

Second, Edwards's knowledge of the Word was matched by his knowledge of the human heart—that dark abyss! To use Edwards's words: "Infinite upon infinite!" So the riddle is this: How can a creature of such infinite sinfulness merit God's favor? How can such a worm even respond to God's grace? How can the dead rise up and walk?

It is noticeable that in his *Personal Narrative,* after a long section on his vile sinfulness, Edwards made this statement: "I have vastly a greater sense, of my universal, exceeding *dependence* on God's grace and strength, and mere good pleasure, of late, than I used formerly to have; and have experienced more of an abhorrence of my own righteousness."[72] This is a striking juxtaposition and gives us a clue as to how Edwards became a believer in God's sovereignty.

This "horrible doctrine" was *believed* by Edwards because he saw no other way for a sinner to be saved. But it was *embraced* by him because it was *God's* sovereignty. And those who *know* their God will trust him and give him all the glory for their salvation.

GLORIA DEI

> *It is manifest, that the Scriptures speak, on all*
> *occasions, as though God made himself his end in*
> *all his works; and as though the same Being, who*
> *is the first cause of all things, were the supreme*
> *and last end of all things.—Jonathan Edwards*

*A*MID ALL HIS LABORS as a pastor, revivalist, and missionary; amid the debates about the Great Awakening and the disputes about communion; amid troubled souls and angry parishioners; Edwards continued to maintain a confidence in the sovereignty of God. He truly believed that all things were under God's control and that God was governing the world for the good of his people.

In a September 1747 letter to Thomas Gillespie (amid much conflict in Northampton), Edwards shared his thoughts on that well-known verse on God's providence, Romans 8:28: "All things work together for good to them that love God." This means, said Edwards, not that every Christian experiences the best of all possible dispensations, or that he experiences the highest possible happiness.

Rather, it means "there is a certain measure of holiness and happiness, to which each one of the elect is eternally appointed, and all things that relate to him work together to bring to pass *this appointed measure of good.*"[73] He elaborated: "The text and context speak of God's eternal purpose of good to the elect, in predestinating them to a conformity to his Son in holiness and happiness. . . . Hence from his reasoning it may be inferred, that all things will tend to, and work together to accomplish, that degree of good which God has purpose to bestow upon them, and not any more."[74]

The sovereign providence of God, therefore, has a view to our eternal place in heaven.

> God, in his government of the world, is carrying on his own designs in every thing; but he is not carrying on that which is not his design, and therefore there is no need of supposing, that all the circumstances, means, and advantages of every saint, are the best in every respect that God could have ordered for him, of that there could have been no circumstances or means of which he could have been the subject, which would with God's usual blessing have issued in his greater good. Every Christian is a living stone, that, in this present state of preparation, is fitting for the place appointed for him in the heavenly temple. In this sense all things undoubtedly work together for good to every one who is called according to God's promise. He is, all the while he lives in this world, by all the dispensations of Providence towards him, fitting for the particular mansion in glory which is appointed and prepared for him.[75]

Edwards's confidence in God's supreme ordering of all things was rooted in his notion that God himself was the ultimate end of creation. In his classic work *Dissertation on the End for Which God Created the World,* Edwards argued that God created the world for the glory of his own name; or, to say the same thing, he created the world for his glory: "For it appears that all that is ever spoken of in the Scripture as an ultimate end of God's works, is included in that one phrase, *the glory of God.*"[76] He explained the latter phrase: "The thing signified by that name, *the glory of God,* when spoken of as the supreme and ultimate end of the works of creation, and of all God's works, is the emanation and true external expression of God's internal glory and fullness. . . . Or, in other words, God's internal glory, in a true and just exhibition, or external existence of it."[77]

God's ultimate end of exhibiting his own glory is not contrary to the blessing of mankind. Indeed, Edwards argued just the opposite: "There is included in this, the exercise of God's perfections to produce a proper effect. . . . The manifestation of his internal glory to created understandings. The communication of the infinite fullness of God to the creature. The creatures' high esteem of God, love to God, and complacence and joy in God, and the proper exercises and expression of these."[78] In other words, the glory of God and the happiness of man are not two ultimate ends; rather, these two ends are one: "These at first view may appear to be entirely distinct things: but if we more closely consider the matter, they will all appear to be one thing."[79]

Edwards's radical God-centered view of reality was at

the root all that he taught and did. He trusted God's providence because God was working all things for his own glory and the good of his people. This vision inspired Edwards to willingly join with God in promoting his glory in the salvation of his fellow creatures. In short, it inspired him with a life vision to consecrate all to the glory of God.

PART 3

THE LEGACY OF JONATHAN EDWARDS

*Edwards is still America's greatest theologian, and
his works remain of lasting value to the church.*
                                   —PHILIP GRAHAM RYKEN

*Now let us look at this man who has had such a
lasting influence, and who seems to be becoming
again almost a dominating influence in religious
thought in America. . . . I am afraid, and I say it
with much regret, that I have to put him ahead
even of Daniel Rowland and George Whitefield.
Indeed I am tempted, perhaps foolishly, to
compare the Puritans to the Alps, Luther and
Calvin to the Himalayas, and Jonathan Edwards to
Mount Everest! He has always seemed to me to be
the man most like the apostle Paul.*
                                   —D. M. LLOYD-JONES

*O what a legacy my husband, and your father, has
left us!*
                                   —SARAH EDWARDS

VINDICATION

*T*HE REAL TRAGEDY OF Edwards's life was not his untimely death by a freak medical accident or the unfinished work he left behind, or (as some historians suggest) his opposition to the spirit of his age. No, the real tragedy of Edwards's life was that he was underappreciated and even mistreated by those he had loyally served. The Northampton dismissal was, as Edwards knew, a blot on his reputation and a shameful example of the blackest ingratitude. It would have been painful enough to be separated from the flock he had served for so many years, but Edwards was dismissed under a cloud of false accusations. A "heap of slanders," as he put it, were thrust upon him, and he lived for many years under the dark shadow of suspicion. Biographer Arthur C. McGiffert observed: "The removal of a minister from his people ordinarily lays him under great disadvantages and commonly hurts his reputation though indeed he be not to blame. There is left on the minds of the world some suspicion, whether something or other blameworthy or unhappy in him, his temper or conduct, was not the cause."[1]

God does, however, honor those who honor him. He vindicates the memory of the righteous. And in Edwards's case, his vindication began before he died. His banishment to Stockbridge proved a boon to both himself and the church. While secluded from refined society, he composed some of the most refined theological and philosophical works ever written. What shortsighted men had meant for evil, God meant for good. In addition, Edwards's appointment as president of Princeton, though brief, was an unsought honor that demonstrated that God had not forgotten him in the frontier wilderness. Although Edwards would have been content to finish his days as a humble missionary, God chose to remove him from a place of exile to establish him in a chair of esteem.

After Edwards's death, the communion controversy continued in New England, and eventually his position on the subject was vindicated. As it turned out, those churches that adopted his position retained their orthodoxy, while those who rejected it became progressively more liberal. As historian J. Tracy has noted: "Every Congregational church in New England, probably, has either adopted that doctrine, or become Unitarian. The future destiny of each of the churches seems to have depended more on its treatment of this question, than on any other single event."[2] It was Edwards's position on church mem-

bership and communion that eventually altered the practice of Congregational churches throughout America.

Moreover, in May 1760, a letter of repentance by
Joseph Hawley Jr., Edwards's chief antagonist, was printed
in a Boston newspaper at his request. It fully vindicated
Edwards.

> In the course of that most melancholy contention with
> Mr. Edwards, I now see that I was very much influenced
> by vast pride, self-sufficiency, ambition, and vanity. I ap-
> pear to myself vile, and doubtless much more so to others
> who are more impartial. . . . Such treatment of Mr. Ed-
> wards, wherein I was so deeply concerned and active,
> was particularly and very aggravatedly sinful and ungrate-
> ful in me, because I was not only under the common obli-
> gations of each individual of the society to him, as a most
> able, diligent and faithful pastor; but I had also received
> many instances of his tenderness, goodness and generos-
> ity to me as a young kinsman, whom he was disposed to
> treat in a most friendly manner. . . . I am most sorely sen-
> sible that nothing but that infinite grace and mercy which
> saved some of the betrayers and murderers of our blessed
> Lord, and the persecutors of his martyrs, can pardon me;
> in which alone I hope for pardon, for the sake of Christ,
> whose blood, blessed be God, cleanseth from all sin.[3]

Years later, Hawley imitated his father's demise: he
committed suicide. Edwards was vindicated.

TO FUTURE GENERATIONS

*T*HE OTHER GREAT CONTROVERSY that engaged much of Edwards's energy was the Great Awakening. To this day, historians are divided, as were the original disputants, over the value of the awakening. This would not have surprised Edwards. Stumbling blocks were inevitable. Nevertheless, much good came out of the revival. It is estimated that as many as twenty to fifty thousand souls came to Christ through the preaching of Edwards, Whitefield, Tennent, and many others. This alone should justify their labors.

Edwards's masterpiece on praying for revival, *A Humble Attempt to Promote Explicit Agreement and Visible Union of God's People in Extraordinary Prayer,* had (and continues to have) a profound influence on the church. As John Armstrong noted:

I think that I can safely say that the little book [*A Humble Attempt*] you now hold in your hands has done more to spark prayer for true revival than any other book in human history, besides the Holy Scriptures. It has generally been understood that a classic is a book judged to be of highest quality over a significant period of time. By this definition, this book is undoubtedly the classic work on the connection of extraordinary prayer to seasons of awakening.[4]

In addition, the evangelistic zeal of the original revivalists spread far and wide throughout the colonies and the Old World. The modern missionary movement was partially inspired by Edwards's own example as a revivalist and missionary, his *Life of Brainerd,* and his revival writings. Both William Carey and Henry Martyn were touched by Edwards's portrayal of Brainerd.

George Marsden noted the missionary and social impact of Edwards:

Through the Civil War era, Edwards' spiritual offspring infused some significant aspects of American culture with Reformed and evangelical concerns. Much of antebellum collegiate education was shaped by New Englanders with Edwardsean heritage. "Disinterested benevolence," popularized by Samuel Hopkins as a practical meaning of Edwards "benevolence to being in general," became a slogan for many evangelists and social reformers. Not only did the *Life of David Brainerd* inspire countless missionaries to lives of self-denial, a similar Edwardsean ideal of sacrificial service was institutionalized in the path-breaking women's school at Mount Holyoke Seminary, founded by Mary Lyon in 1837. Mount Holyoke is best remembered for providing one of the first opportunities for American women to achieve educational parity with men, yet at the time it was equally renowned for the number of its graduates who served as foreign missionaries, described by one historian as "nineteenth-century versions of Jerusha Edwards."[5]

The aftershocks of the Great Awakening were felt also in higher education. Yale gave birth to the modern Student Movement, and Princeton was the home of such Edwardsean heirs as Charles Hodge and Benjamin B. Warfield. Revival became a regular feature of the American landscape, indeed, of the American campus.

Edwards's own descendants were a mighty missionary and social force to be reckoned with in American history. In a work published in 1900, a comparison was done between the descendants of Edwards and those of an unnamed profligate. To quote Marsden:

> The work, published in 1900, contrasted the character and intelligence of 1,200 descendants of one of his most dissolute contemporaries to those of 1,400 of Edwards's heirs. The descendants of Max Jukes, a New York Dutchman whose name the researchers changed to protect the guilty, left a legacy that included more than three hundred "professional paupers," fifty women of ill repute, seven murderers, sixty habitual thieves, and one hundred and thirty other convicted criminals. The Edwards family, by contrast, produced scores of clergymen, thirteen presi-

dents of institutions of higher learning, sixty-five professors, and many other persons of notable achievements.[6]

To be more specific, 173 years after their marriage, Jonathan and Sarah's 11 children produced 13 college presidents, 65 professors, 100 lawyers, a dean of an outstanding law school, 30 judges, 56 physicians, a dean of a medical school, 80 holders of public office, 3 U.S. senators, 3 mayors of large American cities, 3 governors, 1 U.S. vice president, and 1 comptroller of the U.S. Treasury. In addition, Edwards's descendants had written 125 books and edited 18 journals and periodicals. Following the heart and example of Jonathan, nearly 100 of them became missionaries.

LIFE AND LETTERS

*P*ERHAPS THE ULTIMATE VINDICATION of Edwards's life and work is the continued influence he exerts through the written word. Shortly after Edwards's death, Samuel Hopkins wrote a brief biography that he prefaced to the publication of some of Edwards's sermons. He then published the *Two Dissertations* in 1765. In England, Wesley was abridging and publishing *A Faithful Narrative, Some Thoughts on the Revival, Religious Affections,* and the *Life of Brainerd.* Five new titles of Edwards were published in Scotland, and when William Carey was sent to India in 1793, he carried a volume of Edwards with him.

By 1810 a set of Edwards's work was published and had a profound influence on some of the most successful and well-known preachers of the day—men such as Edward Payson, Edward D. Griffin, Lyman Beecher, and others. The latter once counseled his son: "Next after the Bible, read and study Edwards, whom to understand in theology, accommodated to use, will be as high praise in theological science as to understand Newton's works in accommodation to modern uses of natural philosophy." The Scots divine Thomas Chalmers eulogized Edwards's writings:

> There is no European Divine to whom I make such frequent appeals in my classrooms as I do to Edwards.
>
> I have long esteemed him as the greatest of theologians, combining, in a degree that is quite unexampled, the profoundly intellectual with the devotedly spiritual and sacred, and realizing in his own person a most rare yet most beautiful harmony between the simplicity of the Christian pastor on the one hand, and, on the other, all the strength and prowess of a giant in philosophy; so as at once to minister from sabbath to sabbath, and with the most blessed effect, to the hearers of his plain congregation, and yet in the high field of authorship to have traversed, in a way that none had ever done before him, the most inaccessible places, and achieved such a mastery as had never till his time been realized over the most arduous difficulties of our science.[7]

To this day, Edwards's works are being reprinted, read, studied, and discussed by both theologians and philosophers. Even his alma mater, Yale University, which is not now known as a bastion of Calvinism, is publishing a definitive edition of his collected works.

Finally, Edwards continues to influence Christian men

and women by the power of his godly example. While his books are masterpieces of exposition, his life is a masterwork of devotion. From the day of his conversion to the end of his life, he lived in the light of God and eternity. He solemnly dedicated himself to God's glory and conducted his entire life with a view to fulfilling his vow. The key to Edwards is knowing the power of consecration. He gave everything to God: his mind, his body, and his soul. He offered himself as a living sacrifice. He resolved to strive in all ways and at all times to please God. He counted all things as refuse compared to the excellency of Christ, whom he loved above all others. Not content to flicker as a candle, he burned as the sun, giving light to all around him.

Fortunately for us, the divine light continues to shine to this day.

MEMORIAL

MANY TRIBUTES HAVE BEEN paid to Edwards over the years; some we have already noted, and others could be cited. But perhaps the most fitting tribute to close with is the one that now stands over Edwards's grave in Princeton. Etched on the tombstone are the following words:

WOULDST THOU KNOW, OH TRAVELLER,
WHAT MANNER OF PERSON HE WAS
WHOSE MORTAL PART LIES HERE?
A MAN INDEED, IN BODY TALL YET GRACEFUL,
ATTENUATED THROUGH ACIDUITY AND
ABSTINENCE AND STUDIES MOST INTENSE;
IN THE ACUTENESS OF HIS INTELLECT,
HIS SAGACIOUS JUDGMENT AND
HIS PRUDENCE SECOND TO NONE AMONG MORTALS;

IN HIS KNOWLEDGE OF SCIENCES AND
THE LIBERAL ARTS REMARKABLE,
IN SACRED CRITICISM EMINENT, AND
A THEOLOGIAN DISTINGUISHED WITHOUT EQUAL;
AN UNCONQUERED DEFENDER OF THE CHRISTIAN FAITH
AND A PREACHER GRAVE, SOLEMN, DISCRIMINATION;
AND BY THE FAVOR OF GOD MOST HAPPY IN THE SUCCESS AND
ISSUE OF HIS LIFE. ILLUSTRIOUS IN HIS PIETY,
SEDATE IN MANNERS,
BUT TOWARD OTHERS FRIENDLY AND BENIGNANT,
HE LIVED TO BE LOVED AND VENERATED,
AND NOW, ALAS! TO BE LAMENTED IN HIS DEATH.
THE BEREAVED COLLEGE MOURNS FOR HIM,
AND THE CHURCH MOURNS,
BUT HEAVEN REJOICES TO RECEIVE HIM:
ABI VIATOR, ET PIA SEQUERE VESTIGIA.
[GO HENCE OH TRAVELER, AND HIS PIOUS FOOTSTEPS FOLLOW.]

The Lessons of Leadership

✍ A leader masters the body of knowledge necessary in his vocation.

✍ A leader learns the fine art of thinking through study.

✍ A leader's accomplishments are a result of personal discipline.

✍ A leader consecrates all that he is to God.

✍ Leadership requires more than gifts and talents; it demands determination.

✍ Christian leadership transcends the mind and flows from the spirit.

✍ The highest form of leadership will take the lowest place before God.

✍ Love for God is the ultimate motive for sacrificial leadership.

✍ Men follow a leader who genuinely loves them.

✍ Spiritual leadership or ministry must be patterned according to the Scriptures.

✍ Spiritual leadership must follow the example of Christ himself.

❧ Godly civil leadership is a gift of God to society.

❧ A leader's eloquence is a product of his character, passion, and learning.

❧ A spiritual leader must govern his own house well.

❧ A leader's character is shaped by the practice of the spiritual disciplines.

❧ Spiritual leadership demands spiritual discernment.

❧ A leader's confidence rests in God's sovereignty.

❧ A grand God inspires a grand vision.

NOTES

Full bibliographical data can be found in the bibliography.

PART 1: THE LIFE OF JONATHAN EDWARDS

1. Dallimore, *George Whitefield,* 1:413.
2. Ahlstrom, *A Religious History of the American People,* 281.
3. Quoted in Murray, *Jonathan Edwards,* 18.
4. Quoted in ibid., 89.
5. Levin, *Jonathan Edwards,* 95.
6. Edwards, *Works of Jonathan Edwards,* 1:349. Hereafter referred to as *Works.*
7. Ibid., 1:ccx.
8. Ibid., 1:xii.
9. Ibid.
10. "Personal Narrative," in Smith, Stout, and Minkema, *A Jonathan Edwards Reader,* 282.
11. Murray, *Jonathan Edwards,* 26.
12. The Reverend William Williams married Christian Stoddard, Jonathan Edwards's maternal aunt, making William his uncle. The children of William and Christian were William Jr., Elisha, Solomon and Dorothy (Ashley). Hostility developed between the families because the Williams clan was less Calvinistic than the Edwards clan. See ibid., 74.
13. *Works,* 1:xviii.
14. Murray, *Jonathan Edwards,* 31.

15. Ibid., 64.

16. Warfield, *The Works of Benjamin B. Warfield,* 9:530.

17. Edwards, *Personal Narrative,* 283.

18. Ibid., 284.

19. Ibid.

20. Ibid., 285.

21. Ibid.

22. Ibid., 285–86.

23. *Works,* 1:xx–xxii.

24. Murray, *Jonathan Edwards,* 46.

25. Edwards, *Personal Narrative,* 286–87.

26. Ibid., 287–88.

27. "Diary" in Smith, Stout, and Minkema, *Jonathan Edwards Reader,* 268.

28. Murray, *Jonathan Edwards,* 44.

29. Edwards, *Personal Narrative,* 289.

30. Smith, Stout, and Minkema, *Jonathan Edwards Reader,* say July. See 279, n 2.

31. Arminianism was named after James (Jacob) Arminius, who taught theology in Leyden. Originally a Calvinist trained under Theodore Beza, Arminius came to differ with Calvinism on several points. Most notably, he held that God's decree of election was based on foreseen faith and that the extent of Christ's atonement was universal rather than limited to the elect. In Edwards's time, Arminian theology was linked to Episcopalianism, namely, the Church of England, which was governed by bishops (Greek, *episcopos*). The churched of New England, however, were congregational by nature and independent in their church government. In the seventeenth century, rumors continually circulated throughout New England and elsewhere that the king intended to establish an Anglican bishop over the American colonies.

32. Ahlstrom, *Religious History of the American People,* 299.

33. Edwards, *Personal Narrative,* 290–91.

34. *Works,* 1:xxxii.

35. Longfellow, *Complete Poems,* 622.

36. "Faithful Narrative" in Smith, Stout, Minkema, *Jonathan Edwards Reader,* 58.

37. *Works,* 1:cxxxii.

38. Tracy, *Jonathan Edwards,* 20.

39. Murray, *Jonathan Edwards,* 79.

40. Ibid., 89.

41. *Works,* 1:xxxix.

42. "Apostrophe" in Smith, Stout, and Minkema, *Jonathan Edwards Reader,* 281.

43. Murray, *Jonathan Edwards,* 94.

44. Hopkins in Levin, *Jonathan Edwards,* 40.

45. Murray, *Jonathan Edwards,* 312.

46. For a detailed analysis of Edwards as a preacher, see Turnbull, *Jonathan Edwards the Preacher.*

47. *Works,* 1:955ff.

48. See Smith, Stout, and Minkema, *Jonathan Edwards Reader,* 35ff.

49. Murray, *Jonathan Edwards,* 142.

50. *Works,* 2:955ff.

51. Edwards, *Personal Narrative,* 292–93.

52. Ibid., 294.

53. Ibid.

54. Latitudinarians did not insist on strict conformity to a particular doctrine or standard. This tolerance of variations in religious opinion or doctrine was disturbing to Edwards.

55. Ahlstrom, *Religious History of the American People,* 300.

56. *Works,* 2:6.

57. Hopkins, quoted in Levin, *Jonathan Edwards,* 41.

58. Lloyd-Jones, *The Puritans,* 356.

59. Edwards, *Works,* 2:17.

60. Ibid., 1:347.

61. See ibid., 2:620ff.

62. Ibid., 1:347. For information on the Williams family connection to Edwards, see note 12 above and Murray, *Jonathan Edwards,* 74.

63. Ibid., 1:xliii.

64. Ibid., 1:620.

65. "Faithful Narrative," 12–13.

66. Ibid., 24.

67. Ibid., 14.

68. Ibid., 44.

69. Ibid., 37–38, 45.

70. Ibid., 45–47, 72.

71. Gaustad, *The Great Awakening in New England,* 18–20.

72. Murray, *Jonathan Edwards,* 150.

73. Ibid.

74. Ibid., 120.

75. Ibid., 121, notes that "New Hampshire" should read "Hampshire."

76. Ahlstrom, *A Religious History of the American People,* 283.

77. Wesley, *The Works of John Wesley,* 1:160, journal entry for October 9, 1738.

78. In the introduction to "The Distinguishing Marks of a Work of the Spirit of God," in Edwards, *Jonathan Edwards on Revival,* 78 (hereafter, "Distinguishing Marks").

79. Tracy, *The Great Awakening,* 8.

80. Dallimore, *Whitefield,* 493.

81. Ibid., 434–35.

82. Ibid., 481–82.

83. Whitefield, *Journals,* 407–8.

84. Ibid., 421.

85. Murray, *Jonathan Edwards,* 163.

86. "An Account of the Revival of Religion in Northampton in 1740–1742" in Edwards, *Jonathan Edwards on Revival,* 149 (hereafter "Account").

87. Ibid.

88. Ibid., 150.

89. "Sinners in the Hands of an Angry God" in Smith, Stout, and Minkema, *A Jonathan Edwards Reader,* 89–105 (hereafter "Sinners").

90. Murray, *Jonathan Edwards,* 169.

91. "Sinners," 105.

92. Murray, *Jonathan Edwards,* 168–69.

93. "Account," 151.

94. "Distinguishing Marks," 91.

95. Ibid., 109–16.

96. Ibid., 130.

97. *Works,* 1:lxii–lxviii.

98. "Account," 153–54.

99. Ibid., 154.

100. Ibid., 158–59.

101. Ibid., 160.

102. Gaustad, *The Great Awakening in New England,* 36.

103. Ibid., 39.

104. Tracy, *The Great Awakening,* 242.

105. Ibid., 248–49.

106. See Ahlstrom, *A Religious History of the American People,* 285; Gaustad, *The Great Awakening in New England,* 36ff.; Tracy, *The Great Awakening,* 230ff.

107. The French Prophets (also referred to as Camisards) were a group of French Protestants who, during the reign of Louis XIV, rose in arms in Languedoc to restore their church. They were cruelly persecuted in France and some fled to England in 1706. They were know for their charismatic gifts, ecstatic utterances, trances, and prophetic predictions (hence their name). As a result of persecution and a number of failed prophecies, the group scattered across Europe.

108. Murray, *Jonathan Edwards,* 205.

109. Ibid., 238.

110. See sec. 4.

111. "Account," 154–58.

112. Edwards, *The Religious Affections*, 15 (hereafter, *Religious Affections*).

113. Ibid., 120 (emphasis added).

114. *Works*, 1:cxv.

115. Murray, *Jonathan Edwards*, 142.

116. Hopkins quoted in Levin, *Jonathan Edwards*, 44.

117. Murray, *Jonathan Edwards*, 192.

118. Ibid.

119. Ibid., 293.

120. Ibid., 294.

121. *Works*, 1:xci.

122. Ibid., 2:306.

123. Ibid., 2:315.

124. Ibid., 1:xciv.

125. McGiffert, *Jonathan Edwards*, 124–25.

126. Ibid., 125.

127. *Works*, 1:cxcviii.

128. Ibid., 1:432.

129. Murray, *Jonathan Edwards*, 321–22.

130. Ibid., 327.

131. *Works*, 1:cxcviii ff.

132. Murray, *Jonathan Edwards*, 328.

133. *Works*, 1:cxx.

134. Murray, *Jonathan Edwards*, 356.

135. Ibid., 357.

136. Ibid., 363.

137. McGiffert, *Jonathan Edwards*, 146.

138. Murray, *Jonathan Edwards*, 378.

139. *Works*, 1:cliii.

140. Grosart, *Selections from the Unpublished Writings of Jonathan Edwards*, 191ff.

141. Smith, *Jonathan Edwards*, 63.

142. Gerstner, *Jonathan Edwards*, 9.

143. *Works,* 1:125.

143. Ibid., 1:127; see Smith, *Jonathan Edwards,* chap. 6.

145. Murray, *Jonathan Edwards,* 434.

146. *Works,* 1:clxxiv.

147. Ibid.

148. Ibid., 1:clxxv.

149. Ibid., 1:690–91.

150. McGiffert, *Jonathan Edwards,* 212.

151. *Works,* 1:clxxix.

152. Ibid.

PART 2: THE CHARACTER OF JONATHAN EDWARDS

1. David F. Coffin Jr., quoted in Gerstner, *The Rational Biblical Theology of Jonathan Edwards,* 3:605.

2. *Works,* 1:xxxvii.

3. Ibid., 1:xviii.

4. Ibid., 1:xxxi.

5. Austin, *Works of President Edwards,* 4:2 (hereafter *Works (W)*).

6. Ibid., 4:1–15.

7. *Works,* 1:clxxiv.

8. Ibid., 1:xxxviii.

9. Ibid., 1:xxxix.

10. *Works,* 1:xxv.

11. Ibid., 1:xiv.

12. Ibid., 1:xx–xxii.

13. Lloyd-Jones, *The Puritans,* 361.

14. Ibid., 356.

15. Ibid.

16. Warfield, *Works of Benjamin B. Warfield,* 9:515.

17. Ibid., 528.

18. *Works,* 1:xlvii.

19. Ibid., xlvii.

20. Ibid., 1:367.

21. Ibid., 2:14.

22. Ibid., 1:xlvii.

23. Ibid., xlviii.

24. Quoted in Nichols, *Jonathan Edwards,* 55.

25. *Works,* 1:clxxiv.

26. Ibid., xlviii.

27. Kimnach, Minkema, and Sweeney, *The Sermons of Jonathan Edwards,* 5.

28. *Works,* 1:xiv.

29. Ibid.

30. Ibid.

31. Kimnach, Minkema, and Sweeney, *The Sermons of Jonathan Edwards,* 12.

32. *Works (W),* 1:26.

33. *Works,* 1:xviii.

34. *Works (W),* 1:40–41.

35. Edwards, *Charity and Its Fruits,* 3.

36. Ibid., 6.

37. Ibid., 6–7.

38. Ibid., 7.

39. Ibid., 8.

40. Ibid., 9.

41. Ibid.

42. Ibid., 13.

43. Kimnach, Minkema, and Sweeney, *The Sermons of Jonathan Edwards,* 205.

44. *Works (W),* 1:31.

45. Ibid., 3:582.

46. *Works,* 1:clxxxviii.

47. *Works (W),* 3:594.

48. Ibid., 3:605.

49. Kimnach, Minkema, and Sweeney, *The Sermons of Jonathan Edwards,* xxxviii.

50. *Works,* 1:cxxxix.
51. Ibid., 1:clxxxix.
52. Ibid.
53. Ibid., 1:cxc.
54. Ibid.
55. *Works (W),* 1:78.
56. Ibid.
57. Ibid.
58. Ibid., 1:30.
59. Ibid.
60. Ibid., 1:27.
61. *Works,* 1:clxxxiii.
62. *Works (W),* 3:599.
63. Ibid., 3:417.
64. Ibid., 3:434.
65. *Religious Affections,* 266.
66. Ibid., 294.
67. Ibid., 188.
68. Smith, Stout, and Minkema, *Jonathan Edwards Reader,* 283.
69. Ibid.
70. Ibid.
71. *Works (W),* 4:548ff.
72. Ibid., 295 (emphasis added).
73. *Works,* 1:lxxxix.
74. Ibid.
75. Ibid.
76. *Works (W),* 2:253.
77. Ibid.
78. Ibid.
79. Ibid.

PART 3: THE LEGACY OF JONATHAN EDWARDS

1. McGiffert, *Jonathan Edwards,* 133–34.

2. Tracy, *The Great Awakening,* 411.

3. *Works,* 1:cxxv-cxxvii.

4. Moore, *Praying Together for True Revival,* 1.

5. Marsden, *Jonathan Edwards,* 499–500.

6. Ibid., 500–501.

7. Murray, *Jonathan Edwards,* 464–65.

Bibliography

Ahlstrom, Sydney E. *A Religious History of the American People.* New Haven: Yale University Press, 1973.

Aldridge, Alfred Owen. *Jonathan Edwards.* New York: Washington Square Press, 1966.

Bickel, R. Bruce. *Light and Heat.* Morgan, PA: Soli Deo Gloria Publications, 1999.

Dallimore, Arnold. *George Whitefield.* 2 vols. Edinburgh: Banner of Truth Trust, 1970.

Edwards, Jonathan. *Charity and Its Fruits.* 1852. Reprint, Edinburgh: Banner of Truth Trust, 1969.

———. *Jonathan Edwards on Revival.* Edinburgh: Banner of Truth Trust, 1965.

———. *Praying Together for True Revival.* Edited by T. M. Moore. Phillipsburg, NJ: Presbyterian & Reformed Publishing, 2004.

———. *The Religious Affections.* 1746. Reprint, Edinburgh: Banner of Truth of Trust, 1997.

———. *The Works of Jonathan Edwards.* 2 vols. 1834. Reprint, Edinburgh: Banner of Truth Trust, 1974.

———. *The Works of President Edwards, in Four Volumes. A Reprint of the Worcester Edition, with Valuable Additions and a Copious General Index.* 4 vols. New York: Leavitt, Trow & Co., 1844.

Gardiner, J. Norman. *Jonathan Edwards: A Retrospect.* Boston: Houghton, Mifflin and Company, 1901.

Gaustad, Edwin Scott. *The Great Awakening in New England.* 1957. Reprint, Gloucester, MA: Peter Smith, 1965.

Gerstner, Edna. *Jonathan and Sarah: An Uncommon Union.* Morgan, PA: Soli Deo Gloria, 1995.

Gerstner, John H. *Jonathan Edwards: Evangelist.* 1960. Reprint, Morgan, PA: Soli Deo Gloria, 1995.

———. *Jonathan Edwards: A Mini-Theology.* 1987. Reprint, Morgan, PA: Soli Deo Gloria, 1996.

———. *The Rational Biblical Theology of Jonathan Edwards.* Powhatan, VA: Berea Publications; Orlando, FL: Ligonier Ministries, 1991.

Gillies, John. *Historical Collections of Accounts of Revivals.* 1754. Reprint, n.p.: Banner of Truth Trust, 1981.

Grosart, Alexander B., ed. *Selections from the Unpublished Writings of Jonathan Edwards of America.* 1865. Reprint, Ligonier, PA: Soli Deo Gloria, 1992.

Hatch, Nathan O., and Harry S. Stout. *Jonathan Edwards and the American Experience.* New York: Oxford University Press, 1988.

Kimnach, Wislon H., Kenneth P. Minkema, and Douglas A. Sweeney, eds. *The Sermons of Jonathan Edwards.* New Haven: Yale University Press, 1999.

Larsen, David L. *The Company of the Preachers: A History of Biblical Preaching from the Old Testament to the Modern Era.* Grand Rapids: Kregel Publications, 1998.

Levin, David, ed. *Jonathan Edwards: A Profile.* New York: Hill and Wang, 1969.

Lloyd-Jones, D. M. *The Puritans: Their Origins and Successors.* Edinburgh: Banner of Truth Trust, 1987.

Marsden, George. *Jonathan Edwards: A Life.* New Haven: Yale University Press, 2003.

McDermott, Gerald R. *One Holy and Happy Society: The Public Theology of Jonathan Edwards.* University Park: Pennsylvania State University Press, 1992.

————. *Seeing God: Twelve Reliable Signs of True Spirituality.* Downers Grove, IL: InterVarsity Press, 1995.

McGiffert, Arthur Cushman, Jr. *Jonathan Edwards.* New York: Harper and Brothers, 1932.

McNeill, John T. *The History and Character of Calvinism.* New York: Oxford University Press, 1962.

Miller, Perry. *Jonathan Edwards.* 1949. Reprint, Lincoln: University of Nebraska Press, 2005.

Moore, T. M., ed. *Praying Together for True Revival.* Phillipsburg, NJ: Presbyterian & Reformed Publishing, 2004.

Morison, Samuel Eliot. *The Oxford History of the American People.* New York: Oxford University Press, 1965.

Murray, Iain H. *Jonathan Edwards: A New Biography.* Edinburgh: Banner of Truth Trust, 1987.

Nichols, Stephen J. *Jonathan Edwards: A Guided Tour of His Life and Thought.* Phillipsburg, NJ: Presbyterian & Reformed Publishing, 2001.

Piper, John. *God's Passion for His Glory: Living the Vision of Jonathan Edwards.* Wheaton, IL: Crossway Books, 1998.

Simonson, Harold P. *Jonathan Edwards: Theologian of the Heart.* Grand Rapids: Eerdmans, 1974.

Smith, John E. *Jonathan Edwards: Puritan, Preacher, Philosopher.* Notre Dame: University of Notre Dame Press, 1992.

————, Harry S. Stout, and Kenneth Minkema, eds. *A Jonathan Edwards Reader.* New Haven: Yale University Press, 1995.

Stout, Harry S. *The New England Soul: Preaching and Religious Culture in Colonial New England.* New York: Oxford University Press, 1986.

Thompson, C. L. *Times of Refreshing, Being a History of American Revivals, with Their Philosophy and Methods.* Rockford, IL: Golden Censer Co., 1878.

Tracy, Joseph. *The Great Awakening.* Edinburgh: Banner of Truth Trust, 1842.

Tracy, Patricia J. *Jonathan Edwards, Pastor: Religion and Society in Eighteenth-Century Northampton.* New York: Hill and Wang, 1979.

Turnbull, Ralph G. *Jonathan Edwards the Preacher.* Grand Rapids: Baker Book House, 1958.

Walker, Williston. *The Creeds and Platforms of Congregationalism.* 1893. Reprint, New York: Pilgrim Press, 1991.

Warfield, Benjamin B. *The Works of Benjamin B. Warfield,* vol. 9: *Studies in Theology.* Grand Rapids: Baker Book House, 1991.

Wesley, John. *The Works of John Wesley.* 14 vols. Grand Rapids: Baker Book House, 1979.

Whitefield, George. *Journals, 1737–1741.* Gainesville, FL: Scholars' Facsimiles & Reprints, 1969.

INDEX

Ahlstrom, Sydney E., 63
Arminianism, 37, 54, 97

Belcher, Jonathan, 69, 111
Bellamy, Joseph, 97, 113
Brainerd, David, 92–93, 103, 119, 211, 214
Brainerd, John, 113
Buell, Samuel, 78, 80
Burr, Aaron, 110–11
Butler, Joseph, 66

Calvinism, 54, 215
Carey, William, 211, 214
Chauncy, Charles, 83–84
Chubb, Thomas, 108
Coleman, Benjamin, 62–63
Concert for United Prayer, 91
Congregationalism, 37
Cook, Noah, 98

Davenport, James, 80–84, 195
Davenport, John, 81
Deism, 65–66
Dickinson, Jonathan, 60, 93, 124
Doddridge, Phillip, 125

Dwight, Joseph, 105
Dwight, Sereno, 55, 89, 104–5, 132, 134, 159, 183–84, 190
Dwight, Timothy, 104

Edwards, Sarah, 78, 118, 205
Episcopalianism, 37
Erskine, John, 91, 101

Finley, Samuel, 173
Franklin, Benjamin, 68, 70, 83, 143
Frelinghuysen, Theodorus, 68
French Prophets, 83

Garden, Alexander, 69
Gillespie, Thomas, 91, 201
Guyse, John, 63

Hall, David, 99
Hawley, Gideon, 105
Hawley, Joseph, 60, 97–99, 105, 209
Hopkins, Samuel, 46, 90, 94, 113, 160, 168, 184, 188–89, 211, 214
Howe, John, 66, 124

Hulbert, Mary, 95
Hume, David, 125
Hutcheson, Francis, 109

Kellogg, John, 103, 105

Law, William, 66
Lloyd-Jones, Martyn, 144, 205
Locke, John, 27–28, 125

Martyn, Henry, 211
Miller, Perry, 109
Milton, John, 125
M'Laurin, John, 91

Newton, Isaac, 27, 29, 125, 215

Parsons, Elihu, 91, 104, 106
Pemberton, Ebenezer, 60
Pierson, John, 60
Pomeroy, Ebenezer, 98

Robe, James, 91

Sargeant, John, 92, 103–4
Smith, John E., 109
Stoddard, John, 94, 102–3, 178
Stoddard, Solomon, 21–22, 38,
    42–43, 57–58, 68, 89, 94, 97,
    125, 199

Strong, Job, 174

Taylor, John, 110
Tennent, Gilbert, 68
Tennent, William, 60, 68
Tindal, Matthew, 66
Toland, John, 66
Trumbull, Benjamin, 183
Turretin, Francis, 29, 125

van Mastricht, Petrus, 29, 125

Wadsworth, Benjamin, 40, 53
Watts, Isaac, 63, 66, 108, 125
Wesley, John, 20, 64, 67, 91,
    214
West, Stephen, 183–84
Wheelock, Eleazer, 73
Whitby, Daniel, 108
Williams, Chester, 98
Williams, Elisha, 27, 63, 105
Williams, Ephraim, 103, 105
Williams, Israel, 55, 94, 97
Williams, Solomon, 103
Woodbridge, Timothy, 60, 103,
    113
Woolston, Thomas, 66

Zanchius, Jerome, 125